Business Techniques
in
Troubled Times

A TOOLBOX FOR SMALL BUSINESS SUCCESS

THOMAS H. GRAY

Business Techniques in Troubled Times: A Toolbox for Small Business Success

For information about this title, contact the publisher:
Thomas H. Gray Incorporated
5131 Hawthorne Lane
Lisle, Illinois 60532, USA
tgray@tom-gray.com

Library of Congress Control Number: 2013903238

ISBN: 978-0-9886758-0-3

Printed in the United States of America

Cover and Interior design: 1106 Design, Phoenix, AZ. www.1106design.com

Foreword

AMERICA NEEDS THIS BOOK! We need small businesses to succeed, and this book puts the right tools at the fingertips of small business problem-solvers.

America loves small businesses, and with good reason. Small businesses are America's jobs and growth engine. They are crucial for the economic and social health of the local community, and they are living examples of the American dream and American values: economic freedom, self-reliance, and financial success regardless of class or heritage.

Small business owners are motivated entrepreneurs with an idea valued by the market. They are risk-takers but also risk-managers. Above all, small business owners are doers who know very well how to carry out that innovative idea—how to make and deliver their product or service.

While most small business owners are experienced in the *operations* they do, they tend to lack experience in *managing a business*. Occasionally, many need help with management challenges, such as getting financing, setting prices, attracting customers, managing growth, and handling downturns.

Where can small business owners get the advice and training they need? Sources are all around us:

* For no cost, confidential, professional, one-on-one help, small businesses can go to resources like the Small Business Development Centers (SBDC), SCORE, the Turnaround Management Association, and other service providers.

* Networking yields ideas from colleagues.

* The Internet is a gold mine, and bookstores and libraries offer plenty of resources as well.

* Seminars and training courses sell guidance.

* Professional consultants offer fee-based services.

The availability of advice is not the problem. The real issues are "how do I know I need help?" and "what advice can I trust?"

Tom Gray's new book *Business Techniques in Troubled Times: A Toolbox for Small Business Success* is a valuable solution for both these issues. It uses everyday language to show you how to analyze your business so you can see where help is needed. It describes simple ways to solve problems and improve results—a "toolbox" of proven techniques. Plus, the book's modular organization lets you navigate quickly to your issue, like dipping into the toolbox for just the right screwdriver.

How do you know you can trust these techniques? Tom Gray knows what he's talking about! After 30 years of improving results in the corporate world, he's been advising small businesses since 2000. Tom is a certified advisor by the Illinois Entrepreneurship and Small Business Growth Association, SCORE, and the Turnaround Management Association. He teaches business to graduate students at four universities. He started his own consulting firm in 2001 and continues to manage it today.

As a business professional, he has been gathering and refining these techniques for many years. This book finally makes them available to a wider audience, and our communities will be better for it!

The Illinois Small Business Development Centers located throughout the state provide timely information, confidential business guidance, valued training, and access to resources for early-stage and existing small businesses. This book will be one of the resources we recommend.

Mark A. Petrilli
State Director
Illinois Small Business Development Center

Table of Contents

Detailed Table of Contents

Chapter 2: Business Plan and Target Market

Chapter 9: Distributors and Sales Force

Chapter 10: Effective Marketing Communications

"How do I get more customers?" Effective marketing communications makes everything else in your business work. Without it, your business is facing failure.

I have a budget, and I cannot do it all. What media do I spend my money on? Use traditional media to attract people to learn more at your website.

Your website is your front door, your first impression. Use a professional designer, but content is *your* job. Follow this step-by-step approach.

Use social media to monitor the buzz as well as originate valuable content to build relationships leading to sales. Use this step-by-step approach.

Your customer database identifies your best customers, enables more like them, and enables repeat sales. Define your reports, customer record, and entry process.

Suggests twelve reports and how they could be used. Advises on report design, such as a single data element for sorting, linked to the design of the customer record.

Sums up nine articles on marketing planning and effective marketing communications, from business plan to media selection to social media and customer database.

Chapter 13: Process Improvement

Improve contribution margin and profit by reducing variable costs, with process improvement based on a process map.

Improve profits by improved business processes. Consider these techniques: limit options; hand-offs; self-perform; resequence; subassembly/work cell; IT.

After simplifying the process as a whole, improve the longest process steps. Consider bottleneck equipment, methods, process design, metrics, managing people.

Chapter 14: Family Employees

Risks and rewards of hiring family members; tools and techniques for managing family employees in a small business.

Techniques for managing family employees include market-based policies, such as job qualifications and compensation.

For family employees, get accountability by writing down behavior expectations and performance objectives.

Disclaimer

This book is designed to provide information and techniques for starting and managing a business. It is sold with the understanding that the author is not engaged in rendering legal, accounting, or other professional services herein. The author shall have neither liability nor responsibility to any person or entity with respect to any loss or damage caused, or alleged to have been caused, directly or indirectly, by the information contained in this book.

Acknowledgements

THIS BOOK COLLECTS SOME OF the author's experience from over 40 years in business, but one does not gain experience in a vacuum. We are always learning, from those around us and from each challenge we face. I would like to express my deep appreciation for the expertise, opportunities, and fellowship of my colleagues, clients, and students in the corporate world, consulting projects, universities, SCORE, and the Turnaround Management Association.

Like any small business owner, authors need expert advice from time to time. Thanks to all the guest authors and expert advisors listed below for making *Business Techniques in Troubled Times* a *reliable* source for small business owners. I appreciate your interest, your effort, and your time!

Guest Authors
Steve Weihmuller wrote Article 5.2: "Lending in a Community Bank Environment." Steve is Vice President for Commercial Loans at the Community Bank of Wheaton, Glen Ellyn, and a member of SCORE Fox Valley. He can be reached sweihmuller@cbwge.com.

David Gay wrote Article 6.1: "Angel Investors." Dave is Director of the Illinois Small Business Development Center, Center for Entrepreneurship at College of DuPage and has been instrumental in the formation of Collar County Angels. He is a Certified Economic Developer through the International Economic Development Council and Certified Business Development Advisor through the Illinois Entrepreneurship and Small Business Growth Association. Contact Dave at gaydav@cod.edu.

Bill Siniscalchi wrote Article 16.3: "Lessons Learned from an ESOP Exit Experience." Bill is a Certified Mentor at SCORE Fox Valley.

Barb Yong wrote Article 17.4: "Can Small Businesses Benefit from Chapter 11?" Barb is an experienced bankruptcy attorney and a partner in the Chicago law firm of Golan & Christie LLP. Barb represents both debtors and creditors in Chapters 7, 11, and 13. Most of her debtor clients are small- to medium-size businesses and business owners. She also practices commercial litigation and speaks frequently on bankruptcy issues and effective collection techniques. She can be reached at (312) 696-2034 or blyong@golanchristie.com. See *www.golanchristie.com*.

Expert Advisors and Editors

Nancy Gray, Reference Assistant at the College of DuPage Library, led me through using the databases described in Article 2.8: "Market Size: How Many Are Out There?" Nancy is also my beloved wife; without her, nothing works!

Article 5.5 is based in large part on an article in *The Journal for Corporate Renewal:* "Alternative Financing Sources Options for Challenging Situations," Turnaround Management Association, by Tom Goldblatt, CTP, Monomoy Capital Partners, April 2012.

Article 5.6 is based on an article in the *Journal for Corporate Renewal: "Lender Remedies: Reading Between the Lines",* Turnaround Management Association, by Bobby Guy, Attorney with Frost Brown Todd LLC in Nashville, Tennessee, April 2012.

Robert Esquivel, Supervisor of Lender Relations, SBA Illinois District Office, edited Article 5.3: "SBA Loans to Finance Your Business."

Marilyn Huebel, Team Manager, Lending & Latino Outreach Program, Accion Chicago, edited Article 5.4: "Microloans: A Solution for Small Business?"

Chapter 8 on pricing draws on some material presented by Dennis Sester, Phil Grisolia, Mark Purintun, Bill Hess, and the author at the SCORE Fox Valley pricing seminar.

Chuck Fricke, Owner of Turf Masters of Chicagoland, advised on the distributor Articles 8.11, 9.1, and 9.2.

Tim Harlow, Director—US Sales for Bracco Diagnostics Inc., advised on Article 9.4: "Sales Team Compensation Package."

Aimee Grover, website designer and graphic designer, advised on Articles 10.3 and 10.4 about websites and social media. Contact her at *aimee@plaidfish.com*.

Articles 16.1 and 16.2, regarding ESOPs, rely heavily on advice from Robert Schatz, partner, ESOP Plus®: Schatz Brown Glassman Kossow LLP, 1007 Farmington Ave., Suite 4, West Hartford, CT 06107, (860) 231-1054, *www.ESOPPlus.com, rschatz@esopplus.com*, but the author is solely responsible for any errors in properly expressing that advice.

Introduction

EVERY BUSINESS STARTS OUT as a small business. They survive and grow, or die. After three years, half the new sole proprietorships are out of business. New corporations, usually LLCs or S corporations, do better, with a 50 percent survival rate after five years. A third still operate after ten years, and a quarter survive at least fifteen years.[1]

Why is the attrition rate so high for small businesses? Maybe it's because they lack the cash to support the business until it is self-supporting. Maybe it's because their business planning was incomplete or too optimistic. Poor management decisions could also play a role: pricing too low, family employees without the best skills, too much debt, and so on.

Small business owners are "doers." They are pragmatic decision-makers who deal with risk and "figure things out" on their own every day. With the right tools, they will continue to build successful enterprises that make America a better place to live.

This book provides some of those tools. Designed for these "hands-on" owner-managers, it provides and explains practical techniques for solving business problems, putting effective tools in willing hands. The book's structure follows the sequence of the small business experience:

- Business planning
- Getting the financing
- Marketing the products and services
- Managing the operations day-to-day
- Dealing with the outcomes
  - growing the business
  - planning for a profitable exit
  - turning around a distressed business when growth disappears

Each of these "parts" of the book contains one or more chapters, composed of a series of short articles, explaining one or several related business techniques. The articles are practical, focusing on how to use the technique to satisfy customers and improve profits.

This book can certainly be read cover to cover, but it is also designed to be a toolbox, where the reader can select a technique to deal with a current problem. To enable this type of selective usage, a list of article topics follows the Contents page, and a list of techniques per topic follows the Conclusion.

Are there more topics and techniques that could be added? Certainly there are! The brevity of the articles reflects their origin as part of the author's blog, *Business Techniques in Troubled Times*. More articles will be posted there in 2013, such as incentives, performance management, financing moves for distressed companies, new product development, other initiatives for growth, techniques to help sell your business, and others requested by readers.

Readers who find this book useful are welcome to keep up to date with new blog articles, published weekly. You may subscribe to weekly emails of fresh articles at *www.tom-gray.com/blog-2/*.

This past election year makes it clear that our troubled times will continue. We can expect no quick fix. So use this book to keep your business afloat and growing, with proven techniques explained in a practical way!

PART ONE

Strategy and Planning

Strategy and Planning

Business strategy and planning starts with choosing a winning business model, one that fits customer needs and market trends profitably: a "viable core business."

The next step in planning involves thinking through business operations, marketing, and financing to understand the expertise, skills, and effort needed.

Finally, planning also implies that you actually hire or contract for that expertise and those skills, and you gather enough resources so the effort needed is feasible, not superhuman!

In sum, you have a viable concept, and you put yourself in a position to succeed by good planning. If it's important, it's worth planning!

Part One's Driving Concepts

- All businesses start with a vision of what they can become in three years. But vision is not just for start-ups. Every business facing change must reconsider its vision. Stating your vision in terms of the various aspects of the business makes it real and actionable.

* Start-ups with a well-conceived business plan do better, because they know what they have to do, and how much it will cost. Sometimes a good business plan tells the entrepreneur that entry is a bad idea, saving the cost and anguish of subsequent failure.

* The market and marketing sections of the business plan require new ways of thinking for most entrepreneurs, whose strength is producing a great product rather than designing and communicating an attractive offer.

* The business plan includes a realistic view of competitors and how the firm's offering will be different enough to attract their customers.

* The numbers in the business plan help the owner judge the price level needed, i.e., generate cash to run the business and pay off investors/lenders, given a reasonable sales forecast. Too often new businesses charge prices that are too low to survive. If your differentiation is not enough to warrant prices high enough to survive, do not launch the business!

* The marketing, operations, and financial sections of the business plan make clear the skills needed to succeed. Few entrepreneurs have *all* the necessary skills in one person, and the plan is the place where they decide how to gain the missing skill sets.

- The business model is designed for the world as you know it, but that world is sure to change over the years. Sometimes the changes are predictable, but often they are not. A business that will survive for many years will need Part One's vision and planning techniques several times during its life. Successful small business owners have the flexibility to adapt to change and modify their business model.

Techniques Presented in Part One

Topic	Technique	Content	Articles
Vision	Imagining Excellence	Describe company in three years; multiple facets	1.1-1.3
	Gaining Buy-In	Leadership techniques for gaining commitment	1.4
	Nine-Cell Decision Matrix	Prioritization in a group setting	1.5
Business Planning	Business Plan Structure	Simple plan outline	2.1
	Market Analysis	Trends, target market, competitors	2.2, 2.7
	Competitive Analysis and Matrix	Assessing competitors for how well they meet prioritized customer buying criteria	3.1-3.2
	Competitive Analysis, Differentiation and Positioning	Finding and expressing your competitive edge	2.2, 3.1
	Market Sizing	Using databases to profile competitors and size market segments	2.8
	Sales Funnel and Sales Cycle	Realistic views of the sales effort, revenue timing, and sales force sizing	4.1-4.2
	Marketing Planning	Product offers, pricing, sales, communications, customer service to support positioning	2.3
	Sales Forecasting	Methods and mechanics	2.4, 4.2
	Forecasting Cash Flow	Methods and mechanics	2.5, 4.2
	Cash Cycle	Realistic timing for costs vs. revenue	2.5, 4.2
	Presenting the Financial Plan	Summarizing the spreadsheets in your business plan	2.5

Chapter 1: Vision

1.1 Vision Development: The Leader's Role

The vision describes the organization three years from now, answering the question "where are we going?" in a way that makes us want to get there.

Vision is not the same as a mission statement. The mission statement says what the company does for which sets of customers. In contrast, the vision describes what *kind* of company does that and *how well* it does it.

A good vision inspires and motivates employees, provides the basis for goals, and leads to the strategy to achieve them. Most important, it sets the expectations of all stakeholders and aligns employee efforts. Bankers and investors are not the only audience. Employees, customers, suppliers, and the community are all anxious to know what the company will become. They all have a stake in its success.

Even in a small business, the owner needs to decide what success will look like. The owner's vision is the basis for deciding the company's target markets, product development, distribution, technical skills, staffing, and financing. For example, a Product Roadmap (see Article 7.3) implies guidance by a vision of some sort. As the Cheshire Cat famously said, "If you don't know where you're going, any road will take you there."[2]

Why Would We Want to Get *There?*

A good vision *inspires* when it is rooted both in reality and in the values and aspirations of the employees.

* "Rooted in reality" means the vision takes into account both external trends (e.g., technology, demographics, economics) and internal strengths and weaknesses vs. competitors, and takes an objective view rather than wishful thinking. It starts with building the realization that *change is needed*—staying the same is a losing proposition.

* "Rooted in values and aspirations" means the vision describes a company one wants to work for, one that does good and does well at the same time. It has emotional appeal. It says more than "maximize profits."

* To be inspiring, a vision must be positive. It must describe "a better place" we are going to. For example, "beat the competition" or "lower deficits" are negative, while ideas

like "reinvent the industry" and "spread good nutrition worldwide" are positive.

* "Rooted in reality" also means the vision must show a reasonable road to achieve the better outcome. It builds on the organization's culture and strengths. A challenge perceived as impossible is demoralizing, not inspiring.

The literature is unanimous in designating the leader as the one responsible for creating and articulating the vision, communicating it, and gaining buy-in from employees and all the other stakeholders. This applies to leaders of companies, nonprofits, functional organizations, and even nations.

How to Develop a Vision: Team and Form

We know the leader must produce a vision, but how does he or she do it? Does he ascend a mountain alone, hoping to come down with the vision engraved on tablets? Does he look it up on the Internet?

The first technique in developing a vision is to do it as a team. Since buy-in is crucial to a successful vision, a solo approach is not likely to be the right answer. The team who must buy-in must also have a role in developing the vision. The leader can then "create the vision" by leading the discussion and declaring his or her synthesis of the team's thinking.

In addition to "who develops it," the other major question is "what does a vision look like?" Is it a slogan? Is it a cryptic sentence? Is it an elevator speech? Is it as long as a blog post, or longer?

The second technique is to state the vision in both short and long forms. Since a vision describes the company three years from now, a short vision statement (e.g., "the leading widget-maker in the USA") is not clear enough to ensure alignment among the employees. To really communicate, it must be explained by brief statements about various aspects of the company *as it will be* at that future point. See the next two articles for what we mean by "aspects of the company."

A simple, short vision statement runs the risk that each listener will define it their own way, buying in to their own different visions, wasting the opportunity for alignment and setting the stage for future disputes that undermine the focus critical for success.

The next article describes a technique for vision development that has been effective in more than a dozen organizations.

1.2 "Imagining Excellence": A Technique for Vision Development

Every organization needs an inspiring vision to align its efforts and communicate to stakeholders. But a vision only achieves its purpose when it is clearly understood and when the members of the organization all "buy in," that is, they believe it is worth doing and doable. *"Imagining Excellence"* is a proven technique leaders can use to make this happen.

Step One: Orchestrating

The leader must start by accepting the role of *orchestrating* rather than *creating* the vision. He or she gathers and participates in a team of key lieutenants and key contributors or subject matter experts, and together they build a vision of what the company will be in three years.

The leader leads but also listens, and his/her synthesis brings it all together in the end. The people on the team will later be effective communicators because they understand and believe in the vision they helped to build.

These key people are also the ones who can clarify the "short-form" vision by describing the various *aspects of the company* in its future state. See below for more on this.

The leader's first step is to choose the participants and set a date for a two-day off-site meeting.

Step Two: Defining Reality—Why Change?

Second, prior to the meeting, he or she decides what will be needed to *"define reality,"* and appoints people to develop those objective views.

"Define reality" means presenting an external (that is, real) view of the business using the perspectives of people other than management: customers, suppliers, competitors, employees, consultants, investors, or financial analysts. Examples of reality might include new customer research, technology trend analysis, competitive analysis, and financial results/trends.

At the meeting, key lieutenants present these external views first. After this strong dose of reality medicine, the team develops a newly realistic SWOT (chart of Strengths, Weaknesses,

Opportunities, and Threats) and Competitive Analysis Matrix (see Chapters 2 and 3).

Step Three: Short-Form Vision

As they are looking at easel sheets showing their place in the industry, the leader prompts a discussion of "where do we want to be in three years." The result is a draft vision.

Step Four: Long-Form Vision

This is the crucial step. Rather than endlessly wordsmithing the draft vision statement, the team next makes a statement about each of the company's key aspects as they would like them to be in three years. For example, "operations will be able to do X in Y time with Z percent rework."

Some *key aspects* would be product lines, target market segments, competitive position and competitive edge, key competencies, critical processes, infrastructure, supply chain, and sales channels. See the next article for more on these.

To get their attention and make it real, add some general metrics for finance, operations, and sales—not as targets but to help develop a common understanding of the size or extent of the company being envisioned.

Now the meeting gets real. The reality-based "situation analysis" and the draft vision statement might have seemed a bit abstract to a team composed of problem-solvers. In contrast, Imagining Excellence in key aspects is more tangible. It's something they know well and something they have wished for, making it both personal and inspiring.

Step Five: From Vision to Gap Analysis—Old Way and New Way

At the end of the first day, the leader summarizes by extracting "key success factors" from statements about the key aspects of the envisioned company. Then he or she appoints ad-hoc teams to list the projects needed to move these key aspects from where they are today (*old way*) to the vision of excellence just developed (*new way*). The ad-hoc teams do their work overnight after the team dinner or early the next morning, and report back as the second day's meeting begins.

Meanwhile, the leader's overnight assignment is to: 1) ponder what a finalized vision statement might look like, after hearing how the company's key aspects should change, and 2) anticipate the key initiatives and resources needed to move the company from where it is today to achieve the vision.

Step Six: From Gap Analysis to "Major Projects for Change"

The second day's meeting begins with optimistic problem-solvers identifying the gaps between the company today and the company they envision, and proposing major projects or initiatives to achieve the vision.

Improving their functions is what they do best and what they enjoy most. The "can-do" spirit spreads, and inspiration spreads as well. At the same time, the whole team begins to realize what the vision means for the company and for them personally.

After the gap/project reports, the leader and team revisit the short-form draft vision statement, amending it now that they all know what will be needed to achieve it.

Step Seven: Personal Responsibility

Transitioning to strategy, the team moves on to prioritize major projects and appoints a champion for each. A good technique for prioritizing is the Nine-Cell Matrix, explained in Article 1.5. Finally, they select Key Performance Indicators (KPIs) that will measure success in terms of progress toward the vision.

At the end of the meeting, what has been accomplished?

- Common understanding of the company's current and likely future position in the industry
- Vision statement in short form
- Vision statement clarified by a vision for each of the company's key aspects (long-form vision statement)
- Alignment and buy-in among key lieutenant and key contributors
- Prioritization and ownership of major initiatives needed to achieve the vision
- Measures of success

Now the leader can begin the communications and implementation efforts, supported by an aligned team of key people.

Does this seem like a good return on the two-day investment? For a story of how this worked for me in practice, see *"An Operational Turnaround's First 100 Days"* in The Turnaround Management Association's *Journal for Corporate Renewal*.[3]

1.3 Key Aspects of the Company for "Imagining Excellence"

The "Imagining Excellence" technique for developing a vision challenges a leadership team to clarify the vision with statements describing several key aspects of the company three years in the future.

This technique results in a long-form vision statement, enabling all to understand the personal and practical implications of a more cryptic short-form vision statement.

Key Aspects of the Company

Key aspects of the company may include its market position, operations, staff, financial position, and how these are perceived by stakeholders: customers, competitors, suppliers, employees, the financial community, and the local community. Some examples follow:

- Important customers or market segments, and how they perceive the company

- Product portfolio

- Differentiation from competitors

- Competitor perceptions of company strengths and weaknesses

- Market share and sales growth

- Pricing position: leader? discounter?

- Sales channels

- Employee skills and attitudes

- Supply chain

- Major operations processes and quality metrics
- Infrastructure: plant and office facilities, IT systems, other assets
- Organization and governance
- Profitability: margins, cost structure, major cost elements
- Financial structure: cash, debt
- Reputation with investors and lenders
- Reputation in the local community
- Legal and regulatory position

Some aspects will be more important than others depending on the nature of the industry and the draft vision statement. During the vision process, the leader should select no more than ten of these aspects and work with the leadership team to develop a statement describing them in the envisioned company three years in the future.

1.4 Communicating the Vision: Pursuit of "Buy-In"

A vision without "buy-in" falls flat. It fails to inspire, to motivate, and to *align the employees* toward a new and important common purpose. Buy-in is a current buzzword using the images of co-ownership and investment ("buy") to capture the ideas of belief and commitment to vision. Employees who buy-in accept the envisioned outcome as a good thing for the organization, and for themselves as well. Further, they are willing to devote substantial effort to achieving it.

Techniques to Win Buy-In

Winning buy-in is all about communication: words, symbols, and actions. The leader and the leadership team must *communicate their vision* all the time, more often than too often! Techniques include:

- **Broad Participation:** People are honored to be asked to co-develop the vision; later they become convincing communicators in their own networks. They are proud and passionate to be able to say, "I helped define where we are and where we must get to; I helped to define the major projects we need; I am leading or working on an important project team." Involve more people early in the process to create the most widespread buy-in downstream.

- **Personal Explanation by the Leader:** Employees first look to the leader's personal commitment as a model for their own. When they see the leader reach out to them with a simple, honest, and passionate explanation, they feel valued and appreciated, and become predisposed to agree if the leader has credibility.

- **Training:** Applying the vision to each individual work group is the key to buy-in so everyone understands how it can affect them. They need to learn from their boss why change is needed, what the changes will produce, and how that affects their tasks. The buy-in becomes personal when they understand how the changes can make their work more useful, more effective, and hence more satisfying, such as removing obstacles and fostering more cooperative behavior.

- **Everyday Support for Communications and Credibility:** Training is supported by reminders, models, and observations. Post a graphic showing the new vision. Begin new rituals in support of implementation, such as awards or short meetings or a new dress code or fewer privileges of rank. Publicize "heroes" and stories to model the new behaviors. Hire new people with the special skills that have been missing. Provide funding to support new efforts. Pursue "quick wins" and publicize their success to show commitment and gain credibility.

- **Accessible Leader:** The personal presence of the leader in a way that invites employee contact helps win buy-in for two reasons: 1) it creates another opportunity for the leader to reinforce his or her message personally, and 2) it shows the leader's respect for the people who must achieve the vision, by taking time to be with them and listen to their concerns.

Why Some People Withhold Buy-In

See the book *Why Employees Don't Do What They're Supposed to Do and What to Do About It,* by Ferdinand F. Fournies,[4] for an excellent short, common-sense guide for what managers can do to understand and change employee motivations. We can apply its approach to vision buy-in this way:

- **Don't Understand:** I will not buy into a vision if I do not understand why we need to change, and/or why the new goal is better for the company and for me. Solution: define reality, long-form vision, training, and personal access to the leader.

- **Don't Know How:** If you are asking me to do things differently or do different things, show me how. Show me the difference between the old way and the new way. Give me a model. Give me references and reminders. Enable me to practice, and give me feedback on how well I do things the new way.

* **Don't Think the End Result Is Feasible:** People who know what is to be done and why it would be good to do so, and know what is needed to get there, may still feel "we can never become that kind of company because…"

  Listen to these people. Understand the roadblocks they see, and show progress in removing them. Here is where leaders earn their credibility. Refusal to listen says you don't respect your people. Refusal to act on their concerns says you yourself don't understand the company, or you are not really committed because you are not ready to take the difficult actions necessary for success.

* **Don't Agree the End Result Is Desirable:** "Rather than become the envisioned company, we should become something else." The boss must listen and explain the vision rationale as often as necessary, in a variety of ways. Perhaps the vision is a means to an end that could encompass such an employee's dream, or perhaps the vision itself should be altered.

  If neither of these is true, and the employee does not accept the rationale and the vision, then the employee should find another place to work. Failure to act to remove a vision opponent is the worst sort of poor leadership. It undermines the commitment of those who buy-in and reduces the boss's credibility with them.

* **Incentives and Consequences:** "It may be good for the company, but it will not be good for me." The boss must understand the employee's viewpoint and change the incentives to support progress toward the vision. This includes recognition and rewards for doing the right things well, and coaching, potentially followed by negative consequences for working on the wrong things or using the wrong behaviors.

Recognize that the reaction of coworkers is an important incentive. Manage the group's incentives to align them in support of the desired behaviors.

* **Personal Limits:** Employees may not be able to accept new expectations for work hours or travel, or even a move. The boss's first step is to listen and make sure the employee perception is correct. If it is, job redesign or reassignment may be possible. If accommodation is not feasible, the employee should find a different workplace to meet their needs.

Developing the vision is only the beginning of the leader's task. Gaining and retaining buy-in is the real test of leadership skills. It's a test without an end, requiring daily effort by leaders to communicate, listen, reflect, explain, adapt, model, remind, motivate, and act.

1.5 Decision Technique: Nine-Cell Matrix Sorts a Riot of Ideas

Teams involve a number of individuals, so they generate a number of ideas, which all compete for attention and resources—a riot of ideas. To make progress, leaders need a technique to facilitate team agreement on priorities. Waiting for a financial analysis is not the answer, because it kills the team's spirit and momentum. The Nine-Cell Matrix is an effective technique for prioritizing.

Imagine you are leading a group of fifteen lieutenants and key contributors to develop a vision that will describe the company three years from now, or to decide which new products to develop next. How do you bring them together?

Step One: Individuals Assess the Ideas

Let's say all the bright ideas are posted on easel sheets covering the walls of the room. Ask the team to place each of the ideas in the correct cell on their own copy of the following matrix (without the numbers shown; see below for these).

Value	Highest*	Project Project 1	Project Project 1	Project Project 1
	High*	Project Project 3	Project Project 2	Project Project 1
	Medium*	Project Project 4	Project Project 3	Project Project 2
		Low	Medium	High
		Ease of Accomplishment**		

*As one team pointed out, no "low value" ideas are proposed
**Difficulty and cost

Step Two: Assemble Their Assessments

While they are working, draw the matrix (without the numbers) on an easel and distribute pads of Post-it notes. After each team member has completed their own matrix, have them write each idea on a Post-it note and walk up to place them in their preferred cell on the easel matrix.

During a break, write the posted items in each cell on the easel matrix, with the number of "votes" it received for that cell. Then use another easel to draw another matrix and enter your view of the consensus in each cell. Showing the two matrices side by side shows how you considered their "votes" in developing your consensus view.

Step Three: Lead Discussion for Consensus Assessment

After the break, lead a discussion to adjust the consensus view based on shared details and impassioned pleas! Be flexible, recognizing that all this will be tested later with more detailed technical and financial analysis.

When the matrix is finalized, most groups conclude that the projects can be grouped into four priority levels. See the numbers shown in the sample table earlier in this article. The medium value/high ease items are "quick wins." Some of the "2" items may be quick wins as well. The "4" items are rejected, "3" items are deferred, and the "1" items become strategic priorities worthy of significant resources in time and money.

Step Four: Strategy

The resulting prioritized list can be used for the next step: strategy. Since strategy is essentially the allocation of resources, it will be focused on the "1" items. The "3" and "4" items will not receive funding or project development resources. Leaders and managers can then be evaluated on the extent to which they devote their time to the high-priority projects.

Step Five: Personal Responsibility

The team then moves on to assigning owners or "champions" to the high-priority projects. Their first step might be a business case, or a project team and project plan. Thus prioritization enables vision development to move on to strategy.

Chapter 2: Business Plan and Target Market

2.1 Getting Started on Your Business Plan

There are two reasons for writing a business plan: to succeed as a business, and to get a loan or equity investment. The first reason means that *every* new business needs a business plan!

A Business Plan Organizes Your Thinking

Entrepreneurs' minds are a swirling tornado of ideas and questions. A business plan organizes these snippets into a logical sequence. Once you have things in order, you can see the holes, the weaknesses, and the inconsistencies.

For example, one inconsistency would be an ambitious sales forecast without a strong marketing campaign. Another would be a strong marketing campaign without a budget to pay for it.

You wouldn't get very far trying to build a house without a foundation or trying to put on the roof without first building the walls. The same need for sequence applies to planning a business. Putting it all down on paper enables your mind to focus and fill in the holes.

Start with a Simple Business Plan Outline

Dozens of business plan outlines can be found on the Internet, in bookstores, and in software. SCORE has found over the years that this outline works best for start-ups:

1.0 Executive Summary (written last)

2.0 Business and Product Description

3.0 The Market

4.0 Marketing Strategy and Tactics

5.0 Operations/Organization

6.0 Financials

The plan will be ten to twenty pages of text, plus some financial attachments and also some appendix items, used to add detail to items mentioned in your text.

You write the plan in numbered sections, so it doesn't seem like a huge task to tackle all at once. As the old saying goes, "How do you eat an elephant? One bite at a time." The numbering keeps both you and the reader on track.

Draft the Easy Sections First

The easy sections are table of contents (given above), description of the business and products (2.0), and operations/organization (5.0).

Entrepreneurs have the most trouble with the market and marketing sections, and, of course, the financials. So we will cover these in dedicated articles following this one.

You write the executive summary last. It will be a maximum of two pages and should not include any ideas that are not explained in the rest of the text. The best approach is to write summary paragraphs in each of the other sections and tables in the financials section. You copy/paste the summaries and tables into the overall executive summary, and add a few connecting words to make the story flow. This means you really don't have to *write* the Executive Summary at all.

Section 2.0: Business Description (2.1) and Product Description (2.2)

Your business description can be one or two paragraphs. You can use the one below, replacing the underlined items with your own information.

ABC is an Illinois S corporation owned by your name. It is located at address and established in year. ABC provides (type of) products (or services); as such it is part of the XYZ industry, NAIC Code ####. ABC's goal is to provide <u>target market segment</u> (e.g., upscale consumers, or steel processors) <u>with type of product or service</u> (e.g., housecleaning) that is <u>your competitive advantage</u>.

In today's market, these <u>target market</u> customers have difficulty meeting this need, because current suppliers <u>do or don't do what.</u> The benefit to our customers will be <u>what</u> (e.g., save money per purchase or per year; avoid some problem; achieve some missing satisfaction).

This will get you started. You can edit this section later, after drafting the others. For example, you may come up with a different competitive edge after writing Section 3.0. If so, you will want to change 2.1 so the whole plan is consistent on this important point.

The NAIC code—North American Industrial Classification—is available online or at a library with a good business section. Ask the reference librarian. It's used to reference databases to understand how big the market is and who your competitors are. See Articles 2.7 and 2.8, and Chapter 3.

Next, write a *brief* product description (2.2). Limit its length to a half page ideally, or a full page at most. Highlight how it delivers the benefits you promised in 2.1. Don't get into detail on how it works or how you build the product or deliver the service. Those details, if important, can be described in the appendix.

Section 5.0: Operations and Organization

This section shows you have thought through how to produce the product or deliver the service. It also captures your research on the major cost elements that will later be used for your financials. It will be about two pages long. Use bullet items and/or tables rather than long paragraphs.

* Start with the facilities, software/development, and equipment you will need. Say what they are needed for and how much they cost.

* Then list the positions you plan to staff, what their functions are, skills required for each position (to be able to do those functions), and how much they are paid. Be sure to explain what role you will play in operations and why you will be good at that. Your resume or bio can be in the appendix.

* List your professional advisors: banker, accountant, insurance broker, lawyer, and maybe marketing and computer specialist (IT).

* What skills are missing, how will you get them (outsourcing, advisors), and expected cost.

* Key production processes, if any, can be mentioned here. Longer descriptions, or "process maps" (flowcharts), can be in the appendix.

At this point, it's a good idea to start a list of what you plan to put in the appendix so you don't forget.

Now you have a framework. Plus you've written what you know the most about: your business description, your product or service idea, why it's good for customers, and how you will make or deliver it. You can always revise these sections later!

2.2 Describing "The Market" in Your Business Plan—Section 3.0

Effective marketing is the hallmark of a successful business. Its absence means the business will fail. If it is that important, you cannot leave it to chance. You must *plan* how to do marketing effectively.

How Marketing Fits into Your Business Plan

Your business plan is the first place you actually write down those random thoughts about marketing so you and others can see the logic and the holes. Once you figure out the marketing, then you can estimate its cost and include it in your financial plan.

But before you can figure out the marketing, you must figure out the market: who you are going to be selling to. Groups of likely prospects who share certain characteristics are called your "target market."

Describing "The Market"—Section 3.0

To describe the market, you first talk about industry (i.e., all your competitors) sales volume in units and dollars for your target area. Include the sales growth rate. Describe the customer groups (segments) who make those purchases: their demographics, any other characteristics, such as interests or how often they buy, and how many there are in the area. Seasonal ups and downs are also mentioned here. For some sources to measure the size of market segments, see Articles 2.7 and 2.8.

Next you discuss *trends* that might change those industry sales figures or change the ways customers are solving the problem that your product addresses. The acronym DPEST reminds you what trends to think about: demographic, political/regulatory, economic, socio-cultural, technological. When you mention a relevant trend, you will, of course say *why* it is relevant–how it is affecting the current or future market for your product. Your goal is to show that the trend is helping your success—you are consistent with it, not fighting it.

Then you choose the primary segment you will be selling to, and up to two secondary segments. This is your *target market.* Describe your typical customer in each of your target segments. Example: "he or she is (how) old; has X education and Y income; family status is Z; lived in the area for A years; is interested in B, C, and D; and values E, F, and G enough to spend Q dollars on them annually." Now estimate how many of those target customers live in your selling area, using the sources in Article 2.8.

Why bother to identify a target market? Why not sell to all? Effective communications and economical generation of "sales leads" both depend on targeting an audience that has some specific characteristics. These audience characteristics drive the design of your communications plan, the features of your product, your price, and where you sell. You want to spend marketing money reaching those most likely to buy, and buy a lot, and often, not the long shots! So targeting is critical to controlling the marketing budget. It is also critical to crafting a message that is effective by speaking directly to the needs of a specific group of customers.

In the organization of your business plan, industry definition would be 3.1, market trends is 3.2, and target market and its size is 3.3.

Competitive Analysis is Crucial!

Now you move on to a crucial issue for your business: competitive analysis (see Article 3.1). First, describe your competitors, with a paragraph for each. If there are too many, group them into types of competitors so there are no more than three to five. In this description, consider how they are perceived by customers (their "positioning") and how well they satisfy the customer's buying criteria—those five to seven things a customer weighs when choosing a vendor for your product.

After this description of the competitive landscape, summarize it in a table as described in Article 3.2. The table shows how well each competitor meets each of the buying criteria (high, medium, low, or not at all).

Then use the table to evaluate your own offering the same way. Where you are "high" in satisfying customer-buying criteria and others are not, this becomes your *differentiation*—the reason for your business to exist. If there isn't any, don't launch the business! If your differentiation is only price attractiveness, find some extra value to offer that will help you keep customers when competitors lower their prices to match yours. For a brief video on this process, go to *http://www.youtube.com/watch?v=Cgxx9Qf-9wk*.[5]

Now you know who you are selling to and what advantages you offer them compared to your competitors. Your headings look like this:

2.0 Business and Product Description
    2.1 Business Description
    2.2 Product Description and Need Met

3.0 The Market
    3.1 Industry Definition
    3.2 Trends in the Market
    3.3 Target Market and Size
    3.4 Competitive Analysis and Differentiation

Once you know this, you are ready to work on your strategy and tactics for capturing a share of this market. The next article addresses these.

2.3 Marketing Strategy and Tactics—Section 4.0

This is the fun part! Now that you have analyzed the market, chosen a target market, and selected your differentiation, it's time to envision how you will be perceived by the market (positioning) and how you will support that image or slogan with each of the four Ps:

* product

* price

* place (location and distribution)

* promotion (communications)

Later, the market description and these marketing plans will enable you to prepare a well-informed sales forecast.

Positioning

Marketing strategy and tactics start with "positioning." Considering the differentiation you selected at the end of your competitive analysis, create a slogan or catchy statement that says *how you want the customer to think of your product or company.* It will be based on your competitive advantage, but it will be expressed in terms of the *benefits* that advantage delivers to the buyers in your target market.

For example, in its early years Amazon's Kindle e-reader used the phrase "Books in 60 seconds." This is a simple statement of the benefits to buyers resulting from its competitive advantages (differentiations) in the size of its library, the portability of the library within the e-reader, and its free wireless downloads of books. But customers were not buying the size of the library— they were buying books downloaded fast. This was the benefit to them, so it became the "positioning statement."

Later, after tablet computers were launched with e-reader applications and wireless download, Kindle was no longer very different on these features. So its positioning shifted to emphasize its nonglare screen display by adding "read anywhere" to its positioning. Again, buyers were not buying the screen technology for its internal clarity. The benefit they were buying was the opportunity to read on a screen in bright sunlight (i.e., anywhere, even at the beach or on the deck).

Aligning Goals, Strategy, and Tactics

After your insightful positioning statement, the next step is to create the big picture view: company or product goals, the strategy to achieve them, and key tactics to implement that strategy.

Your goals should be specific, both in time and in measurement. For example, "build a presence" is too vague. It would be a good goal statement if you added where, with who, when, and how much, such as "build a presence among Chicago area golfers so that 50 percent are aware of the product and 25 percent express interest in buying it, within two years after product launch."

I like to use a small table to match my goals to the main strategy for achieving them, and make a brief note of the main tactics I'll use to implement each strategy. This keeps me consistent and on track so that my efforts are focused on achieving the goals I started with. Here is a model for you to consider:

Goal	Strategy	Tactics
Build presence in Chicago area in two years: 50% aware; 25% interest	Communication and promotion based on local events and PR	— Communications — Trade shows — Demo days at courses — Order via website
Sell 500 units in year one	Presence in pro shops	— Direct sales — Discounts to sellers — Merchandising
Sell 1,000 units in year two	Presence in retail chains. Introduce complementary new product	— Above plus celebrity endorser — Product Roadmap

This table provides guidance as you consider each of the four Ps, making sure that each one not only supports the positioning but also implements the strategy to achieve the goals. Any activity that does *not* contribute to achieving goals or supporting positioning should *not* be done.

This is what strategy is all about: allocating resources to reach goals. But strategy also means refusing to allocate resources to activities that do *not* enhance the likelihood of reaching goals.

The Plan's Organization

Under the 4.0 heading, state your positioning and marketing goals. The next five subsections (4.1 through 4.5) address the four Ps and customer service. Section 4.6 summarizes your sales forecast.

4.1 Product Plan

You briefly mentioned product features in Section 2.2. Here is where you explain more fully any features that are significant due to difficulty, cost, and competitive impact.

Next, describe the "augmented product": those added features or services that make the entire offering more appealing, different,and valuable (e.g., packaging, choice of paint job, free installation, warranty/guarantee, user manual on a flash drive, etc.).

Third, describe your set of product bundles, often three tiers of product content for three different prices. They might be named basic, standard, and premium, or bronze/silver/gold, but I'm sure you can do better than that! See Articles 7.1 and 8.6 for more on these product tiers, also called packages or bundles.

Fourth, provide a "Product Roadmap" that says what you will do to change the product in the coming months and years. Will there be new versions? If so, what will be the new features? Which market segments are these designed to attract? What technology advances are needed to provide these new features? When can this be introduced? Consider what competitors are likely to offer or respond with. See Article 7.3.

4.2 Pricing Plan

First, show the prices of the product offers (also called packages, bundles, or tiers) and the prices for standalone services outside of these packages or tiers. Ideally, compare the price to the variable cost of the feature and calculate the contribution margin. You will need to do this anyway for your financial forecasts.

Costs/price = margin percentage. Your product margin should be at least 50 percent (i.e., price should be at least twice as much as variable cost). This provides enough cash to cover overhead and still deliver your target profit.

Second, if you did a Product Roadmap, use a table to show price evolution per version over the next two years.

For pricing ideas and methods, see Chapter 8. Consider reactions of competitors to price changes. Will they follow? Can they afford to? What they do influences what you would do next.

Average price per product sold per month is an important input to the revenue (sales) forecast, so it would be good to state your estimate here.

4.3 Distribution Plan

Where will you sell your product? It should be where your target market likes to shop. Also, your choices should be consistent with your positioning: high-end products must be sold at high-end locations. Often you will choose more than one distribution channel to get broader market coverage. This means you will need to deal with price differences among channels:

- *Online:* your website; catalog websites such as Amazon; other special interest sites

- *Retail:* chains, independents, your own stores

- *Distributors and Agents:* add expertise and network of contacts; pay commission or discount
- *Direct Sales Force* for B2B products

For each channel, mention the price discount or commission, and estimate the percentage of total sales this channel will generate. This enables you to calculate sales revenue and costs accurately in the plan's financial statements. See Chapter 9 for advice on distributors and your own sales force.

Describe any significant sales support costs. You incur these costs to generate more sales, by making your distribution channels more effective and more motivated. Examples could range from your website to a portal for distributors as described in Article 9.6. These expenses will later be added to your financial forecast.

Finally, mention any logistics issues and costs involved with getting the product delivered from your location to the selling location.

4.4 Communications and Promotions Plan

What is the message you want to send, to whom, via what media, and what amount or percentage of revenue are you willing to spend? If you have new product offers directed to new target market segments, consider which media would reach them. Most small businesses today depend on their website, social media, local sponsorships and events, and inexpensive local traditional media such as coupons. See Chapter 10 for more guidance on your communications plan.

The timing of communications and promotions should be estimated in this section of your plan, because the effect of these efforts will boost revenue shortly after they begin until they end, and the costs will be incurred before they start until just before they end. These revenue and expense effects must be shown in the financials in the correct months. Obviously, if there aren't any such effects, then the program is ineffective and should not be done!

4.5 Customer Service Plan
Customer service can be important in making the sale, by providing an accessible entry point for questions and by referring prospects to the right channel for closing the sale. Customer service can also be critical for keeping customers and for repeat purchases. So this section of your business plan addresses accessibility, call routing/referral routines, policies for discontented customers, and customer information provided with the sale.

In order to develop accurate financial forecasts, this section will also include the cost of customer service: facilities, staffing, training, and reference materials.

4.6 Sales Forecast
See the next article.

2.4 The Sales Forecast—It's Time to Commit!
Your sales forecast is fundamental to a realistic business plan. It determines profitability. The simplest sales forecast is "units sold per time period," usually per month. If you have more than one product type, you will want to forecast sales of each type separately.

How Do You Estimate Unit Sales for the Future?

Most companies forecast sales by considering several methods, blending the results into something they trust. Here are several common methods:

1. Trended: assumes past sales trends will continue.

2. Bottom-Up: Ask your sale force and distributors to forecast their future sales.

3. Top-Down: Make your own forecast per salesperson or distributor.

4. Market Share: Estimate your share of the market for the year, and then spread those sales across the months considering industry seasonality and your own growth trend.

5. Pace of Growth: Estimate your capacity at business maturity, and gradually grow sales to that point.

6. Customer-Driven: Estimate sales per customer per month. Then estimate a reasonable number of new customers per week or month based on the marketing programs you expect to use. Add them to a spreadsheet row for your new customer additions for each month, and continue to show them in your customer base for as many months as you estimated they would continue to use your services. Remove them when that expires. Customers × unit sales per customer = sales.

Reality Test

Forecasts always need some kind of external benchmark to pro-vide a *reality test*. For example, you could use the sales funnel (see Chapter 4) to test the practicality of a bottom-up forecast.

Consider the sales cycle as well. The *sales cycle* estimates the time between the first customer contact and closing the sale. It may be a few minutes, or six months. If a salesperson is going to make four sales in January, and it is now November, how many accounts should he already be in contact with, based on the normal percentage of contacts converting to sales? Is he on schedule, or will he miss the target?

But There's More!

Once you have a forecast of units sold, the hardest work is done, but you have delivered only a fraction of the information needed. With a little more effort, using either company data or assumptions already in your business plan thinking, you can provide a forecast that is really useful for projecting expenses, profits, and cash flow. You need to forecast each of these in your business plan anyway.

For the most useful sales forecast, the other estimates needed are:

- **Average Price per Product per Month** (average price × units = revenue): This estimate uses the list price minus expected discounts.

- **Sales Commission** is part of your variable costs. Estimate it as a percentage of revenue.

* **Variable Costs per Product** (variable cost per unit × units = variable expenses). Subtract these from revenue to find gross or contribution margin. Use that to calculate breakeven point and to verify that prices are high enough.

* The **Cash Cycle** tells you when cash started to be spent before the sale, such as for raw materials and labor, and after the sale for commissions and shipping. It also tells you when cash arrives as payments after the sale.

For example, you may order raw materials two months before a sale, receive them in two weeks, and pay for them 30 days after that. Thus cash is going out two weeks before the sale. Cash is received at the time of sale in some businesses, or 30 to 60 days later for those companies that use invoicing.

Paying for cash expenses *before* receiving cash payments requires "working capital"—a cash cushion. When it disappears, the business either fails or goes deeper into debt. So the cash flow forecast is probably the most important forecast a small business can make. A short cash cycle means less working capital is needed and success is more likely.

This table shows how each forecasted item is used by the business or in the business plan:

Forecasted Item	Used to Determine			Financial Statements	
Unit Sales by Product	Revenue	Operational capacity needed	Variable costs		
Avg. Price per Product per Month	Revenue				
Revenue				P&L	Cash flow
Sales Commission	Sales compensation planning	Expenses or net revenue		P&L	Cash flow
Variable Costs	Expenses	Gross or contribution margin → pricing and breakeven point	Cash needs	P&L	Cash flow
Cash Cycle	Incoming cash	Cash available	Financing needs		Cash flow

How Do You Capture All This Thinking into Documents?

First, write down your assumptions as you make the unit sales forecast and as you make the other estimates (average price, sales commission, variable costs, cash cycle). A list of key assumptions goes in the financial section of your business plan, and this is a good time to start it.

Second, enter your unchanging sales commission percentage and variable costs per product into Excel cells, and reference these cells in the formulas used to calculate revenue, sales commissions, and variable costs.

Third, set up a new set of rows for cash flow calculations. Assume all sales occur mid-month. Label a row for revenue, a row for sales commission, and a row for each of the variable costs. For each cell in these rows, create a formula to find the cash effect occurring *that* month due to unit sales in *any* month. For example, using the previous example in the cash cycle definition:

- June variable costs = July unit sales for the product $\times$ variable cost for that product (supplies paid for two weeks before sale)
- September revenue = July unit sales for the product $\times$ July price for that product (invoice paid 60 days after sale).

Why Not Just Use Business Plan Software?

Of course, you could also enter your estimates into packaged software such as Business Plan Pro. Then all your numbers would cross-foot, but you would not know how they were calculated because you let the software do it! If you don't know how they are calculated, you will have a hard time managing them. In a small business where "cash is king," it's better to know your numbers intimately if you want your business to succeed.

2.5 Business Plan Financials—Section 6.0

Developing realistic and consistent financial forecasts is one of the main purposes of a business plan. *Presenting* those financials clearly and succinctly is almost as hard as developing them. This article provides some tips for both challenges.

Developing the Financials

Keep a list of the *assumptions* you make while forecasting financial results and the sources you used. Experienced business plan readers will focus on the accuracy of your assumptions before they even look at your forecasts. If the assumptions don't seem reasonable, they will stop reading!

1. Identify all your *start-up requirements*. Research to find likely costs for each.

2. Make a monthly *sales forecast* for the first three years. See Article 2.4.

3. Do a *cash flow forecast* for the first 12 months. This is your tool to figure out how much cash your business needs before it becomes self-supporting. Knowing that, you can determine if you need to borrow money, and if so, how much. See below for direction.

4. Fourth, decide whether you need investors or a loan. If you need money from others, describe *the deal* you want. For loans: amount, when received, interest rate, term of loan, monthly payment, and date you start making payments. For investments, the deal issues are valuation of the business, who has control, and how investors can sell their stake.

5. Develop a three-year *profit and loss statement* (P&L or income statement). This is just an annual total of revenue, major cost categories, and profit. Copy the first year's sales and expense data into the P&L from your cash flow forecast. Then estimate two more years. Don't forget to show loan repayments!

6. Have your accountant prepare a forecast *balance sheet* for the first three years, using the information from these other forecasts.

Sample forms (spreadsheets) for these forecasts are available many places. For example, at *www.scorefoxvalley.org*; see the Resources tab and go to Business Planning.[6]

Monthly Cash Flow Forecast: The Mechanics

Top left: enter cash available before paying for startup costs. Below, enter itemized start-up costs. At bottom, find the cash remaining.

Second column, top: cash available BOP (beginning of period) = cash remaining at bottom of prior column. Enter sales revenue, then variable expenses by type, and then fixed or overhead expenses by type. Second column, bottom, is cash EOP (end of period) = cash BOP plus new revenue minus all those expenses.

This then becomes the third column's cash BOP and so on, just like starting a new page in your checkbook register.

Using the Cash Flow Forecast

Find your "most negative" cash EOP. It will be your largest negative number, usually the last month before you start to show regular monthly positive cash flow.

Then, increase it by at least 15 percent or so, as a "contingency" for unknown costs. This is your protection for not knowing the future perfectly!

The result is the amount of cash you need to start the business. Figure out where to get it. Bank loans are feasible only if you have collateral and you yourself can put up about 25 percent of the amount needed. Microloans are also a possibility. Now go back to item 4 above: define the deal you want if you need a loan. Note: 70 percent of start-ups use their own savings as the main source of their funding.[7]

Presenting the Financials in Your Plan

Your forecasts will be on spreadsheets attached to the business plan. Use five sections to *present* that information in your plan:

- **6.1 Projected Results**

  Present a table with three years of data for unit sales, revenue, variable cost, gross margin, overhead, loan repayment (if any), and profit. Precede the table with some words explaining the conclusion you want the reader to draw from reading the table. You'll copy this into the Executive Summary.

- **6.2 Milestones**

  List the expected dates for major events in business success, such as first sale, first cash flow positive month, first 100 customers, add some facility or staff, etc. Both you and lenders can use these as objectives to measure progress and success.

- **6.3 Financial Requirements: The Deal**

  State the loan or investment you need, the terms you have assumed, and when you expect to begin repayment. Then point to key financials in the 6.1 table to show that there will be ample funds available to repay the loan. Copy/paste this into the executive summary.

- **6.4 Key Assumptions**

  List five to ten assumptions crucial to the most important revenue and expense items. These assumptions must be reasonable for the rest of your plan to be credible.

6.5 Risks and Mitigation

List two to four things that could go wrong and have serious impact on your forecasts. Identify the profit impact for each one (you can rerun your spreadsheets with the bad event replacing your original estimates). Then state your plan to prevent the risk and to minimize its financial impact if it does occur. This shows you are realistic, not just blindly hopeful!

Now reread and edit the plan to make sure all the parts, numbers, and assumptions are consistent.

Then create the executive summary by copying/pasting the summary paragraphs from the important sections. Add a few transition words to link them all into a nice two-page narrative—and you're done!

2.6 Thirty Mistakes to Avoid in Your Business Plan

If you want yourself and your business concept to be taken seriously, avoid these commonly-seen mistakes in your business plan.

Unrealistic Assumptions

1. Market share too high for a start-up (e.g., 10 percent).

2. Starting three lines of business at once, rather than succeeding at one before launching the next.

3. "A low price is the only differentiation I need."

4. "I can personally produce a professional-appearing website and marketing materials."

5. Sales forecast grows at unrealistic pace, uses most of the time of the owner, assumes customers pay right away, and has no source/model from a currently operating business in a similar field.

6. No salary for owner is shown in fixed overhead expenses.

7. Marketing budget is too low.

8. IT budget is too low.

9. No "contingency" for unknowns is considered in the cash flow forecast.

10. Risks are not presented and discussed.

11. "I can get a loan without collateral and without investing 20 to 30 percent of amount needed myself."

12. Timelines assume everything goes well and everyone cooperates according to your desires.

Incomplete Analysis

13. "I have no competition."

14. Your plans for the four Ps do not support the Positioning you chose.

15. Buying new equipment when used versions or leases are available

16. Failure to plan to buy software for bookkeeping, customer data base, order processing, inventory, etc.

17. No recognition or description of key operations processes (hint: if you include flowcharts of these processes in the appendix, you will *really* stand out as a disciplined planner.)

18. Price is too low; contribution (gross) margin is too low; profit is less than 15 percent at maturity.

19. Financials do not include loan repayment!

20. Risks are not described and assessed.

21. No recognition of key skills that are missing or no plan to obtain them.

22. Owner plans to spend almost all of his or her time in operating the production of goods/services, rather than managing the business.

23. Unrealistic timeline to launch, especially if driven by acquiring a particular store location.

Confusing Presentation

24. No page numbers; no outline or section numbers.

25. No "deal" statement.

26. Inconsistencies: text contradicts itself; tables or financials don't add up.

27. No milestones offered.

28. Financials not summed up into a small table.

29. Executive Summary is "creative writing" rather than a summary of the text that follows, or is longer than two pages.

30. Pages and pages of beliefs, philosophies, and values rather than practical tactics for succeeding in business.

What Is the Reader Looking For?

Businesses fail because their differentiation is weak or absent, they fail to communicate it to the target audience (marketing), or they run out of cash before enough prospects hear the message. So your reader is looking for:

- Clear and strong differentiation in meeting a known market need

- Effective marketing plan: message, money, media, timing

- Reasonable sales, cost, margin, and cash flow estimates; nothing too optimistic

- Plans to obtain adequate financing

- Indications that the owner is a good investment: he or she understands how to organize and manage a business, deal with customers, carry out plans as scheduled, keep records, and pay back debts

So write a plan that's as accurate and disciplined as you yourself must be to succeed as an entrepreneur! If you need help, contact SCORE—they've seen it all before. The national SCORE website is *www.score.org*.

2.7 Target Market: Who Are My Customers?

Everybody says you must know your customer, but it's hard to come up with a brief, clear description when a lender or an advertising guru asks you to "describe your target market." What's the value of some abstract definition of your customers? Why make the effort to create one?

Payoffs from Defining Your Target Market
- Reasonable sales forecast so you can budget the amount of money you need

- Reasonable view of the potential size of your business so you are not kidding yourself

- Makes borrowing money feasible; no lender lends until you define your market

- More sales, because your product (and your inventory of companion products) is designed to fit the needs of your target customers

- More sales, because your pricing is designed to fit your target customers

- More sales per advertising dollar, because you select media that reach your target, and your message is directed squarely at what is important to them

- More sales per promotional dollar, because your promotions address their particular needs at the right time

- More repeat customers, because your return and service policies meet expectations

How to Define Your Target Market

Start by describing the personal situation of your perfect customer: he or she is (describe the person) and he or she wants to meet this need (the one your product meets).

Then generalize this description to include measurable "attributes." This enables you to research the size of this target market. Some attributes might be age, income, occupation, family size, gender, location, type of residence, etc. Some might be attitudes rather than demographics. You might even want to include purchase or ownership of something, such as boat or a horse or a motorcycle.

For example, my target market might be adults aged 50 to 70, with incomes over $75,000, within 5 miles of my location who love to dance. Maybe the real sweet spot is male and single as well.

You may have more than one segment in your target market. If so, be able to describe the attributes of each segment.

Once you have the attributes of your target market, you can use databases to find out how many people fit your target market description. See the next article for how to do it. By the way, you can use databases to identify your competitors too!

2.8 Market Size: How Many Are Out There?

Now that you have defined your target market, you can find out how many are in it—your market size.

Data on the size of your market is stored in databases. Those with the most value require a subscription, and the good news is that libraries subscribe for you! Find a library with a good business collection, and then talk to their reference librarian who specializes in business.

A community college such as College of DuPage is a good source. They even offer a scheduled webinar on the Reference USA database. Some (but not all) local public libraries have good business collections, too.

The librarian can suggest the databases likely to have the data you want and can show you how to use them. Usually you will need to have a library card to access the databases online through the library's website, but often you can apply for and get a library card that same day.

One database available without a subscription is American Factfinder (census data), which is available online free. This database (now named Factfinder2) sorts census data according to the attributes you enter. It is much easier to use than *www.census.gov*.

The table below shows nine sources with data you can use to define the size of your target market segments.

Reference USA is great for either identifying other small businesses that are competitors in your area, or for providing the names, size, and contact information for businesses that might become your customers, i.e., not only your target market but a sales prospect list as well!

For example, in DuPage County, Illinois, there are 173 auto top and body repair shops with revenue less than $2.5 million. The list provides the executive's name/address/phone, and the email address for some of them.

The *Encyclopedia of Associations* is listed because associations often have databases of their members and other industry information. You can find the association in this source, and then go to the association directly for their information, or join them to get access to it.

Market Share Reporter can be useful to know what market shares your competitors have, to estimate a reasonable market share for your company to aspire to.

Attitudes, such as "love to dance," can be found in *Lifestyle Market Analyst.*

Household Spending is your source for how many people (of what type) own a particular type of item in your target geography, if this is the key characteristic or attribute of your target market.

You will probably need to use some creativity to interpolate data from more than one database to estimate the size of your target market, but you will be working with real data, not just a hunch!

Sources	Content	Type	Business	Consumer
Reference USA	Yellow Pages; business by type in selected area; contact info; size!	DB	X	
Plunkett's Research Online	Aggregated stats	DB	X	
Encyclopedia of Associations	Industry and other associations	Book	X	
Market Share Reporter	Company market shares	Book	X	
American Fact Finder	Census; segmented by demographics	DB	X	X
Lifestyle Market Analyst	Segmented by attitudes and preferences	Book		X
Household Spending	Who spends how much on what, segmented by behavior	Book		X
Statistical Abstract of U.S.	Everything!	Book	X	X
Direct Marketing List Source	Types of lists you can rent, but it is better to use a list broker rather than order lists on your own	Book	X	X

Chapter 3: Competitive Analysis

3.1 Competitive Analysis and Differentiation: Be Different or Be Gone!

The most important reason to do competitive analysis is to find your differentiation. Every company must have an edge—must be different from competitors in a way that matters to prospects. If your company does not meet customer needs better than other available choices, there is no reason for customers to choose to buy from you.

Without a reason to buy from you, you have no business! Customers will not buy, and bankers will not lend. Bankers will lend only to those companies that seem to be different in a way that matters to customers when they are choosing a supplier.

So your company has to be different. It must enable customers to meet their needs better than if they bought from others. But there is also this other idea—"different in a way that matters."

What Matters to Customers When Choosing Suppliers?

Figuring out what matters to customers—their *buying criteria*—starts with understanding who your target market is, and then understanding their thinking about what they need in your product. For example, when someone is thinking about buying an e-reader, their choices include Kindle or Nook, or a tablet computer with an e-reader app, and perhaps a few other less well-known e-readers. How do they decide what to buy?

They think about (make a mental list of) what the e-reader must deliver. For example, they will want a glare-free display, color display, large library of books (maybe children's books or textbooks?), a reliable unit with decent battery life, a reputable supplier, easy book ordering, protection if things go wrong, and of course, an attractive price considering the value received. For some, other features may be more important than some of those listed above, such as text to speech ("read-to-me").

Humans cannot assess products on dozens of factors. Five to seven is our limit, and maybe seven is too many! Thinking like a customer in your target market group, organize these buying criteria into priority order, and stop at seven (or five). You may want to group some items into a broader category such as "ease of use." This becomes your test list.

Now you will want to talk to some of these target customers and see if you guessed right. Note: don't ask current owners; they know too much! Find people who tell you they are considering buying an e-reader but have not done so yet, maybe at locations where the units are sold, and strike up a conversation. Maybe you can find such research on the Internet, or pay for your own survey or focus group.

Once you have a reasonable set of buying criteria in priority order, then you can assess how well the competitors meet each of these criteria. For those criteria where no one meets them well (no competitor is rated "high"), that is where *you* must be high—*this will be your differentiation.*

Summary of the Process

There is a logical train of thought here:

* You define your target market so you can think like them about their buying criteria.

* Then you assess competitors on those criteria and find your differentiation.

* It is something that matters to prospects because ideally it is one (or two) of their top five to seven buying criteria.

* Having this differentiation, you have a reason to be in business!

* Next you must figure out a "*positioning*" slogan: how you want the customer to think of your company. It will *relate* to the differentiation but *express* customer benefits in a catchy style.

* Once you have your positioning, you can develop your marketing program (the four Ps), where every tactic must support this positioning.

3.2 Competitive Analysis

Once you know your target market's top five to seven *buying criteria* in priority order, you can assess the competition on how well it meets those criteria.

Then you can plan to be different—to be excellent on some criteria that matter to customers where the competitors generally fall short. The final step is to capture your *differentiation* in a marketing slogan or "*positioning*"—what you want customers to think of when they hear your name.

Competitive Analysis in Your Business Plan

Start with two to four paragraphs describing the offerings of competitors today and any improvements they are likely to introduce. In your narrative, be sure to highlight their offering in terms of the buying criteria.

Then set up a table called the *Competitive Analysis Matrix*. You could use the one below and then edit it for your business.

You will have one row for each of the buying criteria and one column for each competitor or group of competitors. Four to five columns is enough. By the way, "price attractiveness" is never the first buying criterion. The first one is most important, so it must be something about how the product meets a need, such as its functionality. After that, people might consider price. If it does not do the job, the price does not matter!

Then, in each cell, enter the consumer's perception (not your perception but what you think is their perception) of how well each competitor meets each buying criteria by entering H (high), M (medium), or L (low).

You will use three extra columns at the right end of the table: common shortfalls, my product, and my strategy.

- Under "common shortfalls," enter an X for a buying criterion where *no* competitor is rated H.

- Under "my product," enter how you expect prospects will rate your product. Be realistic!

- Finally, under "my strategy," enter a word or two saying why you will be better than competitors on that criterion (e.g., "add color").

Review the table to compare the ratings to each other. Modify them if needed to be sure you can explain and defend them. Review the three columns on the right; are your entries accurate?

The last step is to write a short paragraph stating your differentiation from competitors—your competitive edge. Obviously, make sure your words match what the table says. This is why they will buy your product. This is what a lender is looking for!

Positioning

Positioning is a marketing slogan that captures your differentiation and expresses how you want to be thought of by prospects. Your slogan will be positive, expressed in terms of customer benefits. Prospects will think of your company as one that offers value and perhaps good experiences.

Think of several possible slogans and try them out on friends. This is a big decision, because it drives all your marketing, so take your time to find something that makes customers (and you) feel good about your firm.

By the way, always use "price attractiveness" as the buying criteria rather than simply "price." Why? You want all your high ratings to be considered good. High price attractiveness is good, but a high price is bad. So using "price attractiveness" makes all your ratings consistent: high is good; low is bad.

Competitive Analysis Matrix Example

Buying Criteria	Ajax Co	Sell-Co	Big Bertha	Also-Rans	Common Shortfalls	My Product	My Strategy
Performance	M	M	M	L	X	H	Computer Controlled
Durability	H	L	M	L		M	Perf. more important
Price Attractiveness	M	M	L	H	Almost	H	Low overhead
Fit with Other Tools	M	M	H	L		L	Our line will grow
Company Reputation	M	M	H	L		L	Start-up; need references
Order/ Delivery	M	M	L	M	X	H	Web, plus Person option
Easy Training	M	M	M	L	X	H	Online

This table shows a start-up firm whose edge is computer-controlled performance for some type of tool.

- The firm will enter the market as an unknown, supported by references.

- Its appeal (differentiation) will be unmatched performance and attractive pricing for that level of performance, which can save money for its clients.

* It is easy to do business with, but suffers from lack of a broad line of tools that work well together.

* It has also decided to be middle-of-the-road in durability to control costs, believing that its performance advantage will outweigh any durability disadvantage.

* Ajax is competing on durability and a price below Big Bertha. Sellco is a third place firm, and Big Bertha is the leader based on its broad line and established reputation.

A possible positioning slogan: "Cut your costs with the newest cutting edge." This starts with a positive customer benefit and highlights the performance (cutting edge) of our product. It touches on how the customer can reduce his own expenses by using a high-performance tool. For example, there may be no need him to deburr and polish if he uses your machine. It also suggests that your price might be lower than average.

You will want to create your own buying criteria to fit your market and product, but here are some generic criteria to jog your thinking:

* range of products

* quality (hard to differentiate until AFTER one buys)

* selection

* service

* reliability

* stability

* expertise

* appearance or style

* sales method

* credit policies

* advertising

* image

* ease of use

* company reputation

* durability

* fit with other tools

* training requirements

The Competitive Analysis Matrix is a simple tool to sum up the market (customer buying criteria and how well competitors meet them), choose your differentiation, and then your positioning. For a brief video on using this process, see *http://www.youtube.com/watch?v=Cgxx9Q f-9wk.*[8]

Chapter 4: Sales Funnel and Sales Forecast

4.1 Sales Funnel: A Realistic View of the Time and Effort in the Sales Process

The "Sales Funnel" is a classic technique to understand the time and effort involved in making a sale. It's a technique to do a "reality test" on your sales forecast, your estimate of revenue timing for the cash flow forecast, and your estimate of the required number of salespeople.

The sales funnel is a ladder of the steps involved in making a sale, from lead generation through the contact, proposal, negotiation, and sale closing. Like a funnel, its shape is an upside-down pyramid, with the widest layer at the top.

The basic idea is that for each step you have a success rate *less* than 100 percent in moving the prospect on to the next step, so by the end of the funnel, your sales are only a fraction of the number of leads you started out to qualify and contact.

For a good graphic of the funnel, see *http://marketingartfully. com/2011/03/15/small-business-lead-generating-sales-funnel/*[9].

* Leads are opportunities (100 percent)
    o Sales calls make contact (10 percent of above)
        * Follow up with proposal (20 percent of sales calls)
            * Conversion overcomes obstacles (75 percent of proposals)
                o Sale contract (67 percent of conversions)

1. Using the Sales Funnel to Forecast Sales

Start by estimating the "success rate" from step to step. You can fine-tune using experience once you have some! For example,

* 10 percent of leads are qualified and contacted.

* 20 percent of those contacts receive a proposal ("follow-up").

* 50 percent of the proposals become closed sales.

* The other 50 percent fall out during the conversion or negotiation step.

Second, estimate how many leads you expect for the time period. Then work the funnel percentages, and decide if the outcome is reasonable. If not, modify the leads or the percentages.

Finally, you estimate average revenue per sale. Now you can make a reasonable sales forecast—not just dollars, but a forecast based on behavior, so it is more realistic.

2. Using the Sales Funnel to Forecast Revenue Timing for Your Cash Flow

Cash flow is the life of a small business: "Cash is king." For many businesses, cash is not received until weeks after the sale is closed. In the meantime, you need extra cash, called "working capital", to buy supplies, pay people, and otherwise run the business. If you lack this cash, your business can go under. So every business must make it a priority to understand its cash flow.

To figure revenue timing, a critical part of cash flow, you need to estimate the duration of the sales process from lead to close, and then the duration of the production/invoice/billing process.

For example, if it takes two months to make a sale, one month to produce, and 30 days to receive payment, you can expect cash to arrive two months after closing a sale, and four months after you start the selling process. See the next article for a sample.

3. Using the Sales Funnel to Estimate Sales Force Size

The third way to use the sales funnel is to forecast how much "people time" you need to actually make the sales you are forecasting.

Estimate salesperson time required for each sales funnel activity:

- time to qualify the average lead

- time per contact attempt

- number of contact attempts per lead

- time spent in an actual contact (include travel)

* time to create a proposal

* time to negotiate terms

* time to close the sale

* follow-up time by salesperson to ensure customer is satisfied

Then double this, because the literature shows that salespeople spend about half their time selling and half in administration.

Now you can see how much sales time you need to meet your sales target. Do you personally have that much time available for selling? If not, how many salespeople will be needed and what will they cost, or how can you change your estimates to match targets to resources? This is a crucial test of the realism in your business plan.

See the next article for some examples of using the sales funnel for sales and revenue forecasting, revenue timing for cash flow forecasting, and planning the size of your sales force.

4.2 Using the Sales Funnel

In the previous article, we defined the *sales funnel* as a tool for forecasting sales and revenue, revenue timing for cash flow forecasting, and planning the size of your sales force. This article provides some examples for practice.

Example 1: Going *up* the pyramid to see if market is big enough and number of leads needed

	Year 1	Year 2
Revenue (Cash) Goal	$50,000	$150,000
Average Sale	$2,000	$2,000
Sales Needed	25	75
Success Proposal to Sale (50%)	50	150
Success Contact to Proposal (20%)	250	750
Success Lead to Contact (10%) (7,500 vs. market size?)	2,500	7,500

Example 2: Sales/Cash cycle for first 25 sales

Sales Cycle: 3 Mo. to Sell, 1 Mo. to Perform, 1 Mo. to Pay	Mo. 7	8	9	10	11	12
Sales	2	4	8	11	13	15
Revenue Booked after Job Completed/Invoiced (Avg. Sale Is $2,000)		4K	8K	16K	22K	26K
Cash Received 1 Month after Invoice; 2 Months Post-Sale			4K	8K	16K	22K
Total Cash						50K

Note: you need enough start-up cash to support your business expenses until cash begins to come in.

Example 3: Salesperson Time Required in Year 2 of Example 1

Task	Time for Each	# to Do	Total Hours
Attempt to Contact Lead	5 minutes	7,500	37,500 mins/60 = 625
Make Contact	1 hour	750 (10% of leads)	750
Write Proposal	2 hours	150 (20% of contacts)	300
Negotiate	4 hours	100 (67% of proposals)	400
Close Sale	4 hours	75 (50% of proposals)	300
Total Time			2,375
Your Time @ 20hrs/Week			1,000 Shortage = 1,375

Example 3 shows that your sales forecast is unrealistic unless you add one or two salespeople, or you spend more than twenty hours per week selling. If you don't, your revenue flow will be less than half your forecast, and you will run out of cash before the business can turn a profit. Don't be this guy!

Financing Your Business

PART Two assumes your business plan shows how much financing you need, including a contingency for the unknown. You've decided to invest your own funds for at least 25 percent of the business's needs. You have assembled a clear business plan showing the uses of funds and how they will be paid back.

Now you need to raise the money. How do you do that? Chapter 5 addresses lending. Chapter 6 discusses some equity investments.

Part Two's Driving Concepts

- To get money from others, you must be an attractive investment. Your business idea must have differentiation. You must have evidence of the skills to run a business, good credit and character, collateral, and enough cash to invest 25 percent of the amount needed.

- You must also *look* like an attractive investment. Your business plan must be logical, complete, well-organized, and well-presented. It should pass the "Thirty Mistakes" test in Article 2.6. You should be aware of all the skills needed and should have a believable plan to get them.

* Plan for adequate profits with adequate prices, and then ask for enough money! Many small businesses require as long as two years before they generate enough profits to recover their start-up costs as well as cover day-to-day operational costs. If the business plan is too optimistic, start-up funds will fall short and cash will run out during these first two years.

* Choose the right type of loan and lender. What loan type fits your needs and collateral: traditional loan, SBA-guaranteed loan, microloan, alternative financing (if already operating)? What lender fits that loan: community bank, active SBA lender, nonprofit doing microloans?

* Consider angel investors if you have the right type of business, expect major growth, and are willing to give up some control and share in future value.

* Treat family investors professionally, with a written agreement covering control and exit.

Techniques Presented in Part Two

Topic	Techniques	Content	Articles
Financing with Debt	Becoming an Attractive Borrower	Resources; loan uses; are you a good risk?	5.1
	Community Bank Lending Criteria	Goals; banker's basic questions/ criteria; documents needed	5.2
	SBA Loans	Top SBA lenders; eligibility; loan types/terms	5.3
	Microloans	Lenders; size and terms; eligibility and uses; peer-to-peer lending	5.4
	Asset-Based Lending (ABL)	Types of collateral; interest rates; sources	5.5
	Understanding Lender Remedies	Early, middle, and late stage lender techniques and borrower responses	5.6
Financing with Equity	Understanding Angel Investors	Who are angel investors; what types of businesses; terms; other benefits; sources	6.1
	Investing with Family	Business plan analysis: bases for assumptions; working capital; profit distribution; valuation	6.2
	Managing Risk in Family Investment	Types of risks; shareholder agreements; supermajority rights; dispute resolution; exit provisions	6.3

Chapter 5: Loans and Lenders

5.1 Financing Your Business

"How can I get the financing I need" is probably the most popular question among entrepreneurs. Maybe you have an attractive business concept, but it takes some financing to get started. Or maybe you have an operating business with plenty of customers willing to pay for the value of your products, but you need some cash to grow the business or recover from setbacks.

To understand types of financing, see "*15 Sources of Financing*" for a simple two-page list provided by SCORE Fox Valley.[10] The most typical methods for start-ups are personal savings, friends and family, home equity, credit cards, and leasing equipment.

Note: 70 percent of start-ups use their own savings as the main source of their funding.[11]

Loans are also feasible, but they all require some personal cash input, often about 25 percent of your total financing needs. Loans also require collateral and a personal guarantee of repayment. If you are already operating a business and need to grow, other options become available.

By the way, you don't see grants listed above because grants are generally not available to "for-profit" businesses. For more information on grants, see *SCORE on grants*.[12]

Lenders Consider How You Will Use the Loan

Most financiers are NOT interested in providing funds for survival, such as paying routine supplier bills or other debts. Instead, they look for clients who will use their funds for growth. "Growth uses" include creating collateral (such as buying assets) and/or growing the cash generation capability of the business with new products, new markets, or new capabilities. Growth uses include working capital to enable purchase of raw materials for your growing volume of orders.

Why would they be so "picky" about how the money is used? It's all about being paid back. Common sense tells them that "growth uses" provide better assurance that the loan or investment will be paid back with an appropriate return (interest or profit). In contrast, "survival uses" do not change the fundamentals of an underperforming business (i.e., the reason it could not survive on its own cash flow in the first place).

That type of business is an unacceptable risk for profitable payback of standard loans. However, "alternative financing" or equity investments may be available for such firms, because both of those approaches provide the investors with greater returns to compensate for higher risk.

Am I a Good Risk?

This leads to thinking about what it takes to attract someone to give you money to develop your business. Potential lenders are interested in assured payback; potential investors are interested in likely profit. They seek a profit big enough to be worth the risk of investing in a small, unknown business, compared to the profit they could get from investing in the stock of more well-known entities. For example, the Dow Jones Industrial Average gained 9 to 10 percent annually since 1900.

This means they want to understand both you and your business well enough to have confidence that their investment will pay off. First, they will want to understand you, because unreliable management (that could be you!) can destroy even the most promising business.

What do they want to know about you? First, your character and personal reliability; second, your resources; third, how well your skills fit the role you will play in managing the business.

Personal Character: Evidence of your character and personal reliability starts with your personal credit history: credit rating, past bankruptcy, and status of your payments on current loans. The next consideration is whether your personal and business tax filings are up to date. They may also look into other matters such as criminal record or other publicly available information.

Your resources are important because lenders will require that you supply a significant percentage of the business's total financing requirements, usually around 25 percent. If you do not believe in yourself and the business enough to invest substantial funds, then how can you expect anyone else to believe and invest?

You will also be required to provide collateral for any loaned amount, as well as your personal guarantee of repayment. So lenders will want to make sure that you have these funds and assets available. A natural response is, "If I did have them available, I would use them instead of the loan." If you have these resources, you should indeed consider whether you need a loan or not, because loans can be expensive.

Skills fit role? The other personal issue is your skills vs. the role you have assigned yourself in the business. Your business plan should have already identified the types of skills needed to succeed and where the business will get those skills. In the plan, you have assigned yourself a role, usually as the overall manager. If your role is to run the business, the bank will want to know whether you have ever done that before successfully, ideally in the same industry. If not, how can they be assured you can do it now?

The right approach to minimizing management risk is to assemble advisors and other managers who have the skills you are missing, and describe in your business plan how this team will work together.

After lenders are satisfied with your personal risk profile, then they consider the prospects for the business itself. They will be looking for a *coherent business plan,* including marketing and operations, milestones, and most important, industry trends and averages that show your own financial projections are reasonable. If you have an operating business already, they will also look at your current debt vs. cash flow to see if the business can support more debt repayment.

For start-ups, a good source is *"Can I Qualify for a Loan?"*[13] For an operating business, more detail on loans and the information required to obtain them can be found at *"The ABCs of Borrowing."*[14] Both articles are from the Score Fox Valley website (Resources tab).

5.2 Lending in a Community Bank Environment

By guest author Steve Weihmuller, Vice President, Commercial Loans, Community Bank of Wheaton, Glen Ellyn

This article provides a community banker's perspective on funding new loans. It has gotten tougher to get and tougher to provide funding over the last several years. However, we bankers are still lending, and the basic principles have never changed. Commercial lenders really do like to make loans; really, we do like to lend money. In fact, at the community bank level, this is one of the few ways we can make a profit and, therefore, keep our doors open.

Since the recession, we have had a couple of different layers of approval added to the already difficult maze called "underwriting," the industry term for deciding whether the risk/return on a loan request is acceptable. This was needed based upon how the markets had operated before and during the recession. The pendulum of finance swings high, either tightening and or loosening based on the economic view of the nation and the community in which we live.

Commercial lenders are responsible for helping to grow the bank profitably. The only way I know how to do that, as a commercial lender, is to take care of clients, help them with their financial needs, and attract additional clients along the way. As a lender there is nothing more satisfying than helping someone succeed. When the client wins and the bank grows together with the client, it makes all the inevitable paperwork worthwhile. We all look for that symbiotic relationship that is win-win for both parties. OK, enough of trying to justify my professional existence. Let's get to the brass tacks: what my underwriters and the federal government (who insures your deposits) are looking for when reviewing a loan request.

The Basic Questions

You need to be clear on each of these questions before you pick up the phone to call. Who? What? Why? When? Where? How? Remember, I *want* to lend you the money. What you say here will make me want to continue the conversation, become skeptical, or politely let you know that I cannot help you. Do your homework. By having your basics worked out, you will save everyone time. Your time is valuable; don't waste it.

Questions the underwriter has to answer in order to recommend an approval:

If I put the money out, will it come back? • Cash flow of the business (Always keep in mind that "cash is king") • Liquidity • Net worth • Gross and net profit margins • Do you know your breakeven numbers?
If the cash flow dries up, is there a secondary source of repayment? • Collateral • Liquidity • Guarantor/coborrower • Global cash flow
Credit history? • Have previous creditors been paid back? • Is there a lot of unsecured debt (credit cards not paid in full monthly)? • What sort of credit score do you have?

For what purpose? Would you want to lend your money for this purpose?
• Turn-down answers:
  o Cover previous losses
  o Pay personal expenses
  o Buy gold
• Approval Answers
  o Add staff to help with increasing demand
  o Buy equipment to cover increasing demand
  o Working capital to help cover the increased receivables

Who are we lending to? • Character; your resume counts • Have they ever done this before? • Does the purpose make sense? • What on the resume or past experience makes you think this will work?

Yes, I know, "That's a bunch of stuff to answer just for a couple of bucks." That's kind of the point; as a commercial lender, for a community bank, I am looking for more than a transaction.

I want a relationship. The good part is it actually gets easier as we get to know each other better. The bad part is that the underwriter will still ask me for way too much information but, with all the i's dotted and the t's crossed, the presentation will be completed and ready for approval. My job is to add color and context, based on what you've told me as well as my own experience, to make the underwriter want to approve your request.

Business Documents: Cash Flow and P&L Results

Remember your audience: bankers and underwriters. For a new business, an Excel spreadsheet showing where and how the cash flows will be generated is essential (two years minimum). For an operating business, a two-year future cash flow spreadsheet is also required, but it must be provided together with the last three years of the business's financial history. This information is taken from the last three years' tax returns and/or internal financial statements of the business.

Nobody cares what you did three years ago unless results show a trend going down. If that happened, explain the reason and what you did to correct it. If the trend is up, life is good but the underwriters will still ask why? So be ready to explain how your brilliant management style has motivated employees and customers and kept sales and net income trending up.

Lending at community banks is alive; it still has a cold but is getting better every day. With the right advocate, your commercial lender, you can navigate the maze and find the dough.

For more information, contact SCORE, your accountant, or your local community banker.

5.3 SBA Loans to Finance Your Business

An SBA loan is *not* an alternative to a bank loan. The Small Business Administration (SBA) helps businesses get started and grow, not by lending taxpayer funds directly, but by *guaranteeing bank loans* against loss. This is intended to make the bank more willing to lend to a small business with few assets and little history.

The SBA offers to guarantee up to 85 percent of the loaned amount in return for upfront charges (similar to a bank's "points") and a competitive interest rate, both paid by the borrower. The guarantee fees normally cover *all* the cost of the SBA administration and loan losses so that taxpayer money is not involved.

What Bank Should You Use?

Banks like the guarantee because it reduces their risk and because the bank's requirement to hold funds in reserve does not apply to the guaranteed amount. This means the bank has more funds available to make other loans, which is how it makes money. However, offsetting these benefits are two negatives: the bank cannot charge points for an SBA loan and the process of executing the SBA loan guarantee is considered a burden by some banks.

As a result, not all banks will process a loan to obtain the SBA guarantee. Active SBA lenders solve that complexity issue by having an expert on staff who manages the process. Small business owners seeking an SBA-guaranteed loan should apply to a bank familiar with SBA loans for two reasons: the bank itself does not need to be persuaded that the SBA loan process is manageable, and the bank's familiarity with the process means that it will be executed more quickly than by other banks. Note: the bank will want all the borrower's banking business, not just the loan.

The top SBA lenders nationwide can be found on the SBA's website at *www.sba.gov.* The top eleven in Illinois for 2011 are shown below.

Bank	# of SBA loans	Total Amount Guaranteed
JP Morgan Chase	519	$64,660,400
Ridgestone Bank	172	$144,106,100
Associated Bank	98	$16,872,700
US Bank	91	$56,173,600
Charter One	66	$6,892,000
Superior Financial	55	$627,000
First American Bank	42	$13,723,400
Wells Fargo Bank	38	$18,996,000
Fifth Third Bank	31	$8,694,200
Rockford Bank	29	$7,715,400
First Colorado National	28	$33,826,000

Other Illinois banks that are highly active in SBA loans include the Wintrust banks and Resource Bank.

Am I Eligible?

While the SBA has its own types of loan guarantees and its own underwriting standards, the first step in getting an SBA-guaranteed loan is that the bank itself must be interested in lending to a particular borrower for a particular purpose. Remember that the bank itself is responsible for at least part of the loan risk, because the SBA will not guarantee the entire loan. This means that all the advice in Article 5.2 about getting a bank loan still applies, even if you are seeking an SBA loan.

Assuming the bank is interested in financing you and your business and the bank agrees to your request to seek an SBA guarantee, the next step is to understand the SBA *eligibility* rules and types of SBA loans to see which fits you best. Note that the limits stated here are subject to changing government rules.

- Eligibility—Definition of Small Business:
  - Retail or service: up to $7 million in revenue
  - Manufacturing: up to 500 employees
  - Wholesale: up to 100 employees
  - Annual profit: up to $5 million

- Eligibility—Use of Funds (Purpose):
  - Assets: land and/or buildings; expand/convert existing facilities; machinery/equipment
  - Working capital: supplies, materials, inventory, long-term working capital
  - Short-term asset-based line of credit
  - Debt refinancing under limited circumstances

What Kind of Terms Can I Get?

For those who are eligible, the SBA's main loan guarantee types and terms are presently:

Type	Max Loan	Max Guarantee	Max Term	Interest	Fees as % of Guarantee
7 (a)	$5M	>$150K = 75% <$150K = 85%	10 yrs, or 25 yrs for real estate	>7 yrs = prime + 2.75% <7 yrs = prime + 2.25%	>$700K=3.5% $150-$700K=3% <$150K = 2%
SBA Express	$350K	50%	Same as 7(a)	Same as 7(a)	Same as 7(a)
Patriot Express*	$500K	Same as 7(a)	Same as 7(a)	Same as 7(a)	Same as 7(a)
Export Express	$5M	>$350K = 75% <$350K = 90%	Same as 7(a)	Same as 7(a)	Same as 7(a)

*For veterans or their spouses

"Express loans" are the most popular these days. The attraction is that you do not need SBA documentation or to wait for SBA approval. Only the lending bank's application is required.

The prime rate in late September 2012 was 3.25 percent. The spread (amount above the prime rate) varies by length of loan, type of collateral, and adjustable rate terms of the loan.

In addition, the SBA offers a 504-type loan guarantee of up to 40 percent of the project for Certified Development Companies. (See the SBA's website for details.) SBA also offers Microloans (see the next article).

So what is the winning strategy for a speedy loan? Select an SBA-experienced bank, place all your banking business with them, fill out their application, convince them that you and your business are attractive, and ask for an SBA Express loan. Compare its terms with the bank's own terms, if there were no SBA guarantee. Use SCORE for advice in the process.

SBA contact info: www.sba.gov; phone: (312) 353-4528

5.4 Microloans: A Solution for Small Business?

For those who don't need a large loan, the paperwork and underwriting process for a normal bank loan seems like overkill. Fortunately, the financial community and the Small Business Administration (SBA) agree. Small loans involve less money at risk, so they should require less lender effort, but the traditional bank underwriting process was designed for larger loans. Microloans offered by nonprofits, such as Accion, can be the solution to reducing the processing cost while still controlling risk.

Who Is Involved?

Microloans are targeted at low-to-moderate income business owners with a business plan, collateral, a cosigner if required, and the ability to self-provide at least 10 to 20 percent of the money they need. Microlenders generally offer loan products that range between $250 and $50,000, though in some areas of the country, the maximum amount may be larger, with specific guidelines on what they fund and maximum amounts for start-ups. These are mission-driven organizations that must balance their mission—helping entrepreneurs—with appropriate financial rigor to satisfy investors and regulators.

Accion is an alternative lending organization dedicated to providing credit and other business services to small business owners who do not have access to traditional sources of financing. They handle 90 percent of microloans in the Chicagoland area and estimate they are meeting only 10 percent of the need. Accion is part of a 50-year-old global organization and has been lending in Chicago since 1994. It is also a member of the Accion US Network, the only microlending network in the country.

How Big Are Microloans, and What Are the Terms?

At Accion in Chicago, the maximum loan for a new business is $20,000. Their average microloan amount is about $8,000; the national average is $13,000. The maximum term of the loan is six years, with interest rates ranging from 8 to 13 percent according to the SBA, and 8.99 to 15.99 percent at Accion. These rates are generally higher than rates charged at a bank but lower than a credit card.

Accion also has two reduced interest rate loan programs, such as one for businesses in selected counties. There is no prepayment fee for paying off the loan early, and the pre-payment option can minimize the interest costs incurred, but there is a closing fee that is added to the loan principal. Normally Accion disburses the cash within fifteen days of receiving a completed application with all the required supporting documents. See *Small Business Loans : Financial & Business Advice : Accion East and Online* and *Microloan Program | SBA.gov.*[15]

Am I Eligible?

Does this sound made to order for you? Consider the eligibility requirements and acceptable uses of the funds before deciding.

Accion Eligibility Requirements	Acceptable Uses of Funds (Purpose)
• Borrower is the business owner or co-owner • Strong commitment to business and repayment • Willing to invest personal funds for 10 to 20 percent of amount needed • Clean or improving payment history with creditors • Age 21 or more, or 18 with cosigner • Business plan, one year of cash flow projections; brief plan if loan is $4,000 or less; SCORE can help! • Industry experience and alternate source of income if start-up • Collateral, including all personal and business assets (includes cosigner's guarantee)	• Buying a qualifying business (up to $20K) • Not nonprofit, real estate development, exporting, multilevel marketing, lending, adult entertainment, weapons sales, or illegal or polluting activities • Normally not for debt repayment • Working capital (includes marketing) • Inventory and supplies • Furniture and fixtures • Machinery and equipment

Disqualifiers include outstanding tax liens, unless you are on a repayment plan; active bankruptcy; delinquent mortgage, rent, or child support; or multiple recent charge-offs and delinquencies. Credit scores and history are considered on a case-by-case basis.

In 2011 Accion Chicago made 301 loans, with 40 percent to women and 75 percent to minorities. Accion also provides small "credit-builder" loans up to $2,500 to those with damaged or no credit, as well as financial education workshops and one-on-one counseling to small business owners. Ninety-two percent of Accion Chicago's clients are still in business two years after receiving the loan, and 89 percent of its clients repay their loans on schedule.

So if you are a good borrower, you have a business plan, and your business needs start-up money or funds for marketing or a vehicle or shop improvements, a microloan may be right for you. Contact SCORE for free advice as you create that winning business plan, at *www.scorefoxvalley.org/* (Chicago suburbs, outside Cook County) or *www.scorechicago.org/* (Chicago and Cook County).

Peer-to-peer lending, also called "crowdfunding," is a relatively new category of microloans. Two service providers, Prosper .com and Lending Club, were launched in the mid-2000s "with the idea of letting [mom-and-pop] investors make small loans directly to consumers. Borrowers would pay less interest than they would on typical credit cards, while lenders would get higher returns than they would in other yield-producing assets, such as government bonds," according to Joe Light of the *Wall Street Journal*.[16]

These loans are unique in two ways: the loans are *unsecured* by collateral, and credit rating standards can be less than banks require (e.g., a 640 credit score). They are similar to other microloans in most other ways: a maximum amount of

$25,000 to $35,000, an average loan amount near $6,000, a maximum term of five years, and an origination fee (points) of 0.5 to 4.5 percent.

Interest rates for these peer-to-peer loans, which depend on credit rating, range from 7.4 to 23 percent or even 28 percent for the riskiest borrowers.

5.5 Asset-Based Lending: An Alternative to Bank Loans and Microloans

Lenders charge interest rates and usually require some kind of collateral: valuable assets that they can take over and sell if the loan is not repaid on time. The exceptions are called "unsecured loans," those requiring no collateral. They usually involve smaller amounts and higher interest rates due to high risk to the lender, because the lender has no recourse if the borrower does not pay it back as agreed.

Two forms of unsecured loans are credit card debt and peer-to-peer lending (see Article 5.4). The other source for an unsecured loan might be friends and family. See Articles 6.2 and 6.3 for some advice on investing in a family business.

Alternative Lenders Have Different Views on Collateral

Banks, being risk-averse, have fairly strict rules on the types of collateral they will accept: real estate, machinery in place or other "hard" assets, and cash accounts. But there are alternatives to banks—lenders that have a more flexible view of acceptable collateral.

This is called *asset-based lending or ABL*. Unlike a bank loan, ABL loans may be secured by business assets whose *value changes over time*. Examples include a machine that is being purchased, a major purchase order, raw materials inventory, work-in-progress inventory, finished goods (as yet unsold) inventory, and accounts receivable. The purpose of such loans is to provide the working capital to enable the business to bridge the time lag between spending on production and receipt of payment.

ABL Can be Quick But Costly

The amount of asset-based loans "can be up to 85 percent of accounts receivable and up to 60 percent of inventory."[17] The form of such loans can be an ordinary term loan or a revolving line of credit that is paid off and renewed as the secured collateral evolves. ABL interest rates are higher than bank loans but less than credit card debt. The time required for approval of ABL loans can be quite short. Their purpose can include refinancing as well as ordinary business operations.

Factoring Your Receivables

"Factoring" is another form of ABL, usually applied to accounts receivable. This involves actually selling the asset—the accounts receivable—for less than face value to a lender that then collects from those customers over time. It can be especially attractive "when domestic banks will not lend [on foreign receivables] due to credit risk, country risk, and exchange rate risk."[18] The downside of factoring, aside from a discount or interest rate, is reputation risk. Customers may lose confidence in the firm and refuse to place additional orders due to concern for its financial stability.

Borrowing on Intellectual Property

Another asset ignored by banks but considered by alternative ABL lenders is intellectual property or IP: patents, trademarks, or copyrights. An *intellectual property loan* can generate cash without actually selling either the IP itself or a stake in the business. Aside from the interest rate, the issue with IP loans is how to value the intellectual property, which is why it is not feasible for start-ups. In fact, most ABL is not available to start-ups, with the exception of *purchase order financing*.

Source and Summary

ABL involves higher interest rates due to greater risk, but there are plenty of companies in the business. For example, Fisher Enterprises (*www.fisherenterprisesLLC.com*) is a New York-based clearinghouse representing several hundred nontraditional money sources—generally nonbank lenders for amounts from $50,000 to $500 million. Fisher charges a retainer for the company's efforts, which is credited against a 1 to 3 percent success fee at closing.

While bank loans remain the lowest-cost form of debt financing, alternative financing in the form of asset-based loans is available to going concerns needing a capital infusion to finance growth and operations and willing to pay for it.

5.6 Failure to Repay as Agreed: Lender Remedies

Prior articles in Chapter 5 have been about getting loans. There have been no articles yet on paying loans, because your lender will be sure to tell you how to do that! However, sometimes borrowers do not pay back loans as agreed, for lots of good and sometimes bad reasons. All borrowers need to know what lenders might do in that situation, just in case you have to face it.

Lenders have many techniques available. Think of them as early, middle, and late stage remedies.[19]

Early Stage Remedies

Early stage remedies are designed to get the attention of the defaulting borrower so that the situation does not get worse, and to buy time for both parties to work out a solution, such as replacement financing.

The lender starts the process by sending a notice letter, reserving its rights to more severe action in the future, and perhaps activating terms of the lending contract. These might include:

* certain number of days for the borrower to "cure" the default

* higher default interest rate

* prohibition of payments to equity holders, affiliates, or subordinated lenders unless approved by the lender

The result of negotiations at this early stage could be an agreement waiving the lender's rights (forbearance) and providing the borrower with an extension, often for a fee or a higher interest rate or a pledge of additional collateral.

Middle Stage Remedies

If the parties do not agree to modify arrangements in the early stage, then middle stage remedies can come into play. These are designed to provoke immediate action by the borrower but still leave room for a negotiated solution. They may enable the lender to begin recovering some of the debt, while avoiding costly action by the bank to take over the business or the collateral.

After a default, the lender usually has the right to "call" the loan—to sue for the entire amount of the principal and unpaid interest, rather than merely sue for any overdue payments. There may be a default fee as well. This may also apply to leases. This lawsuit will be against anyone who guaranteed the loan, as well as the business itself. Lawsuits have deadlines, which increases the pressure on the borrower.

Other middle stage remedies include canceling a related line of credit, requiring that the borrower hire a turnaround professional as a condition to grant forbearance, and sending in auditors to review the borrower's books (cost paid by borrower). The audit team's report also estimates the value of the company and suggests the best ways for the bank to recover its money using late stage remedies.

Late Stage Remedies

When the problem reaches the late stage, there is little hope for resolution and the remedies are all about recovering the lender's funds by taking over collateral. The borrower's response may be to declare bankruptcy (either to liquidate or to reorganize), which has the effect of forestalling ("staying") the lender's efforts to collect. See Article 17.4. If there is no bankruptcy filed, the lender can sell the collateral to the highest bidder. Even in a bankruptcy, the lender can bid for the assets of the company using the amount it is owed as part of the cash amount of its bid (called "credit bid").

However, the lender may wish to keep the assets functioning and earning cash. If so, there are several ways it can take over control of the company and its operations. The lender may ask the courts to appoint a receiver to run the company for the benefit of the creditors, or even advance funds to the company to enable it to keep operating (debtor-in-possession financing, or DIP), thus protecting the value of its collateral.

In addition, it is becoming more common for the borrower to pledge its stock in the company as collateral for a loan. If that is the case, then in a bankruptcy the lender will become the controlling shareholder as well as the leading creditor, and control the company through its shareholder rights.

Lenders may also decide to simply sell the loan at a discount in order to be rid of the complexity and cost of enforcing their rights. In that event, the buyer of the distressed debt will have all the same rights that the lender had and likely will also have less patience and more expertise in operating distressed businesses or dealing with their managers.

Conclusion

To sum it up, don't let your loan get into a default position. Keep your promises and pay your debts. If that cannot be done, then react *early* to the default and find a solution in the early stage, whether you are a borrower or a lender. Otherwise, the cost goes up and the result gets worse as the process goes on.

PART TWO: FINANCING YOUR BUSINESS

Chapter 6: Angel and Family Investors

6.1 Angel Investors

By guest author David Gay, Director, Illinois Small Business Development Center

Who Are Angel Investors?

In a simple sense, they are individuals who see potential in your business model and are willing to invest "patient" money with the expectation that they will be rewarded in the longer term based upon the business's success. They also understand that their entire investment can evaporate if the business fails.

What does an angel investor look like? Well, it could be family and/or friends. Let's face it, if they are willing to invest some cash in your business with delayed repayment terms, they are indeed angels: people investing in the business based upon the faith and confidence of the owner (entrepreneur) and the business model. If the deal goes bad, well, that can certainly lead to some uncomfortable Thanksgiving dinners, but on the other hand, they won't foreclose on your house, car, and first-born child as a bank or lender would do.

Legally, angel investors are individuals who meet certain financial criteria as established by the Securities and Exchange Commission under Regulation D. They are required to have a net worth over $1 million excluding personal residence and/or annual income of $200,000 ($300,000 for dual income households) for the past two years, with reasonable expectations that this will continue. In other words, angels must be people who have sufficient financial resources that they can lose their investment and not devastate their personal situation.

Further, they are individuals who have an appreciation for entrepreneurial endeavors. They've been entrepreneurs themselves or appreciate early-stage opportunities in new technologies or market penetration.

What Types of Businesses Do Angels Invest In?

Angels may invest as individuals or may cluster in groups. Angel groups pool their money for investments in deals that meet their criteria in terms of industry type, stage of development, investment limits, and other parameters. Some angels or angel groups invest in prerevenue/early-stage ideas, while others will only consider businesses that have realized sales, achieved profitability, and are looking to expand their markets or product lines. It all depends upon the appetite of the individual(s).

Are angel investors right for your business? It depends on your type of business. Individual angels and angel groups do not invest in "lifestyle" businesses, so if you are looking at opening the next great restaurant, retail store or consulting firm, your angels will be limited to the aforementioned family and friends.

Typically, angels are looking for new technologies or other business models that can tap into a large potential market, grow quickly without major transformation (scalable), and retain their competitive advantage during and after growth. These will be business-to-business models. Attractive technologies include bio-tech, nanotech, health-care devices, software, and others.

What Are Their Terms?

A "typical" angel investment level is generally between a couple hundred thousand and couple of million dollars—the latter generally requiring several individual investors to pool their money under one investment structure. The terms of the investment might seem severe to many entrepreneurs, as angel investors are looking to cash out of their investment to the tune of ten times cash within a three to seven year time frame, so you can see that market potential and scalability are critical.

This ten times cash-out translates to an annualized rate of return near 50 percent for a single project, but the likelihood of failure with early-stage investments is so great that this generates an annualized return of only 15 to 20 percent on the angels' entire portfolio. For example, if the portfolio includes ten ventures, typical outcomes could be three failing totally, three never quite making it and requiring more and more cash transfusions, three becoming self-supporting, and one shooting star whose spectacular returns carry the entire portfolio to the 15 to 20 percent target return.

In considering whether angel investors are right for your business, you must assess the size of your market and the ability of your business to grow quickly. For example, if you convince the angel(s) to invest $500,000 in your business today, how do you intend to cash them out to the tune of $5 million in about five years? Usually the scenario for payback involves the technology being proved out, markets developed, and a larger organization buying out your company.

One might now ask, "What's the difference between angels and venture capitalists if both groups are expecting such large returns on their investments?" It is a matter of scale in one sense. Most venture capital groups make larger investments, with $2 to $3 million being on the low side. Also, venture capital is typically professional management of pooled (other people's) money, while angels are investing their own funds and/or joining with others who are also using their own funds.

What Else Should You Know about Angel Investors?

Angels bring more than money to your business. Angels tend to invest in businesses and industries that they understand so they can bring managerial experience to the table and help make contacts, open doors, and provide guidance that can prove valuable to the developing business.

There are some excellent resources out there on angel investing. For further information, you might look to the Kauffmann Foundation at *www.entrepreneurship.org/en/Resource-Center/Topics/Accounting-and-Finance.aspx* and/or the Angel Investor Association at *www.angelcapitalassociation.org/*.[20]

For those readers in the West Suburban Chicago area, please note that a new angel network of and for DuPage and the Collar Counties has been in the formation process for the past year. We have been working closely with Dr. Ron Kirschner, founder of Heartland Angels, in connecting with prospective angel investors, advising the group on structure, and sharing knowledge Heartland has gained over the past ten years. The group has not yet set its target industry/size/stage profile. Contact the author, Dave Gay, for more information.

6.2 Family Investment: Risk and Protection

A brother-in-law, cousin, or uncle asks you to "help him out" by investing in his new business venture. It happens every day and can work out to mutual benefit, but many times this does not end well. Why doesn't it? Why the old saying: "gain an investor, lose a friend"? What can you do to protect yourself and still help out? The issues can be summed up as start-up planning, valuation and form of investment, control, and exit.

Consider this example: Your cousin is an experienced franchise manager and has a new franchise opportunity in another state. He needs $275,000 to get it going. He will put up $200,000 in the form of a loan to the business, secured by mortgages on the rental buildings he owns and his personal guarantee. You are asked to invest $50,000 cash for 12.5 percent ownership. The person who will be the manager, who has worked as such for your cousin before, will invest $25,000 for 6.25 percent ownership, and her stake is expected to grow in future years.

Start-Up Planning

* How much cash does the business need to get started, and what will it be used for?

  – Typically, this will be worked out in a *business plan*. Ask to see it. Ask for more information on the assumptions that were used to do the financials. If they were based on the cousin's previous franchise's results, ask to see those records to verify those were really the results. If they are industry averages, ask for the source. President Reagan famously said, "Trust, but verify."

* Is there enough working capital and enough in the bank in case the business plan projections are overly optimistic, or should you expect to be asked to invest more cash soon after start-up?

  – This should be in the business plan financials and related assumptions.

* How much are the profits, how much is your share, and when can you expect to receive your returns?

  – This should be in the business plan as well.

Valuation and Form of Investment

* What is the rationale for valuing the business at $400,000? This is implied if your 50K is worth one-eighth or 12.5 percent of the business. Why not value it at $325,000, since that is what is being invested now? Then your $50,000 would be worth 15 percent ownership.

  – The cousin should provide industry (or franchisor) data showing the value of similar franchises in the area at different times in their development.

* Is your cash worth the same, dollar for dollar, as a loan to the business guaranteed by the cousin? If so, shouldn't the cousin's ownership be no more than 5.5 times yours?

  – Probably not, if the cousin is also going to contribute experienced management and you are a passive investor not involved in day-to-day decisions. That experienced decision-making has value, and in return for providing it, your cousin gets a higher percentage of ownership.

* There is also a manager aside from your cousin. Why would her stake rise over time, and will this cause your stake to decline over time, or will the cousin's stake decline, or both? Will she invest cash or some other value to earn that future growth in her stake?

  – The business plan should say how the venture will be organized (e.g., LLC, S corporation, C corporation or partnership, etc.). *Rules for changes in ownership* should be written in the LLC operating agreement, the S corporation's bylaws, or the C corporation's shareholder agreement. Every investor should be satisfied with the terms in this agreement before investing money. This document gives you legal recourse; verbal assurances are harder to enforce.

* Would you prefer to invest by lending $50,000 to the business in a promissory note, rather than sending cash for shares of stock? If so, you would earn a stated rate of interest rather than dividends (if any). You would also get a monthly principal repayment, *if* the company was not short funds from lack of business or perhaps due to excess salaries paid to the other two owners for their operating efforts! When the loan comes due, you would be paid

before any profits were distributed to others but after any bank loan was paid.

However, as a nonowner, you would *not* get the percentage of profits matching your stake, you would *not* get a share of the proceeds when the business is sold, and you would *not* have any say in the decisions made to control business results.

– You should *hire your own legal and investment advisors*, rather than depending on your cousin's. You need advisors who are watching out for your own interests. Other forms of investment are also possible, such as preferred stock, or investing in some business asset via an LLC rather than investing in the business as a whole. Your advisors can explain!

In summary, before investing, insist on a business plan and an agreement specifying shareowner rights and duties. Satisfy yourself that the business plan is reasonable, based on verifiable assumptions. Use your own advisors to help you decide whether the shareowner agreement is fair to you, or whether you may be more comfortable making a loan rather than an investment.

6.3 Family Investment: Control and Exit

Before making an investment in a relative's business, be sure to negotiate and write down how business decisions will be made (in terms of how you can or cannot control them) and how the business will handle the exit of any investor or the entry of a new investor.

Solving these questions at the beginning avoids emotional and time-sensitive pressures when the event actually happens. Making good decisions under those circumstances is more difficult than handling the issue at the outset in a shareholder or operating agreement.

In the previous article, we used the example of investing $50,000 in a cousin's new franchise for 12.5 percent ownership, with a 6.25 percent owner gradually increasing her stake until it is twice as large as yours. That article addressed risks in the areas of start-up planning and valuation/form of investment. This article considers risks of control and exit.

Control Risk

As a 12.5 percent owner, you have a minority interest, your cousin has the majority with 81.25 percent, and the manager has 6.25 percent. If decisions are made by majority vote, with majority defined as majority of the shares, you will never be able to control a decision. Your influence is limited to your charming personality, depending on the empathy and good faith of the other investors.

- Operational decisions will be made by the manager under the supervision of the cousin, both of whom are experienced in the business. Examples are pricing, product, advertising, process design, choosing suppliers, and so on.

  - Do not expect to participate in those decisions. Risks include bad judgment and kickbacks. If you do not have confidence in their business judgment and ethics, do not invest.

- Other decisions may have greater direct impact on the value of your investment. Examples might include:
  - taking a major loan
  - buying a company
  - taking on or buying out an investor
  - a call for more capital investment from current investors
  - replacement of a key manager
  - signing a major new contract (e.g., with the franchisor)
  - accounting controls to prevent embezzlement

- In the shareholder agreement, you will want to specify the types of major decisions where you need a veto right to protect the value of your investment. The technique is called a *"supermajority" voting requirement,* meaning that approval of that type of decision requires a "yes" vote from more than 50 percent of the shares.

A reasonable outcome is that the majority shareholder must get one other minority shareholder to agree with him so the supermajority voting requirement would be his 81.25 percent, plus the manager's 6.25 percent = 87.5 percent, or even 82 percent. Some states may define a minimum set of such decision types in their incorporation laws, but usually you can go beyond their definition if you prefer.

- If you believe that the manager may be unduly influenced by the cousin, you might try for agreement on 93.75 percent as the supermajority voting requirement. This means your cousin must have *your* agreement on these major decisions. This would be your veto right. Consider also the gradual increase of the manager's stake and how that might affect supermajority voting percentages.

- Supermajority voting requirements allow owners of minority stakes to prevent business actions. The resulting impasse may diminish the value of the business and thus cannot be allowed to endure. Many companies provide some resolution for the impasse, such as the majority owner being able to buy some or all of the minority owner's shares at a predetermined valuation.

Exit Risk

"Exit" happens when an investor sells his shares. In our example, you may want to sell your stake, or the majority owner may want to sell his. In a small business there will be no public market for the shares, so the business itself usually buys out the exiting owner. Arrangements for buying out an owner should be in the shareholder agreement when the business is formed.

* If the business is the buyer, how will the shares be valued?

    - The agreement will often say "at market value," as defined by an independent valuation expert, or three of them: one chosen by the company, one by the exiting shareowner, and one chosen by these other two.

* Where will the business get the funds to make the buyout?

    - Sources may include a loan, cash investment by other shareowners, purchase by an Employee Stock Ownership Plan (ESOP), or a loan by the exiting investor himself. Note that when an investor dies and the estate wishes to sell the shares, often the business has the funds because it bought life insurance on all the major investors for just this purpose.

- What if the business does not execute the buyout?

  — Usually the agreement gives the business a "right of first offer" to buy the shares, but that expires after a stated number of days, enabling the exiting owner to find a buyer wherever he can. The remaining investors may fear co-ownership with an unknown buyer and may not want to engage in a bidding war with a potential other buyer, so they usually make the buy offer within the deadline or get the seller's agreement to extend it.

One other clause in the shareholder agreement is *dispute resolution*. Here the parties agree at the outset how they will settle disputes over whether the agreement has been violated, and if so, how to resolve the breach. Issues here are mediation vs. arbitration vs. lawsuit and responsibility for selection and fees of mediator or arbitrator.

In summary, before investing, be sure to verify the business plan and negotiate a fair shareholder agreement with your lawyer's advice. Plan ahead for disputes, for control of decisions affecting your investment's value, and for buyout of your stake when you want to exit.

Effective Marketing

Effective Marketing

IN ADDITION TO GOOD PLANNING and adequate financing, effective marketing is the third key to business success or failure.

Part Three's Driving Concepts

* Marketing is not just communications. It includes product variations, pricing and discounts, where the product is sold (location), communications, and customer service.

* Product tactics should include three tiers of packaged services, added services (augmented product), and a Product Roadmap.

* Pricing depends not just on competition. Prices need to be high enough to cover overhead (fixed expenses) and generate the necessary profit. There is no point in setting prices that win unprofitable sales! Too many entrepreneurs ignore this fundamental goal of pricing. They are either unaware of the overall financial results of their business or are simply afraid to charge more than competitors, even

when their differentiation would still attract customers. Fewer customers at a higher profit is a road they are afraid to take. The result is stumbling along until they run out of cash to support an unprofitable but dearly loved business.

* Sales succeeds with the right compensation and the right sales support. Distributors add value, but you must attract them with the right deal.

* Once you have a good story to tell (products, pricing, attractive location), then the key to sales is communications and customer service that brings back repeat purchasers. In today's world, communications begins with the Internet. You will need web and social media marketing skills. You will also be using traditional media, often to attract prospects to your website. Your business plan must provide for these skills and their costs.

* No one can perfectly predict the effectiveness of a marketing or communications initiative, so effective marketing depends on tests and revisions to find which approach has the best results. Thus marketing takes time and attention, creativity, and then adaptability. It is not something that can be considered every now and then. Entrepreneurs focused on operational excellence fail without the communications that attract new and especially repeat customers.

As the business develops, watch for changes in the market, attend to your marketing, and understand your overall financials—especially pricing—to build a sustainable profit-making enterprise.

Part Three considers the four Ps in the classic sequence: product, pricing, place (who sells where), and promotion (i.e., communications).

Techniques Presented in Part Three

Topic	Techniques	Content	Articles
Product Strategy	Three Tiers	Bundles of features	7.1
	Augmented Product	Packaging; warranties; ancillary services	7.1
	Service Design	Design the customer experience according to positioning	7.2
	Product Roadmap	New product schedule according to customer segment needs	7.3
Pricing Strategy	Summary of Techniques	Summary and brief description of ten techniques	8.1
	Pricing Objectives	Value positioning and target margin	8.2
	Margin Analysis	Methods and mechanics	8.3
	High List Price	Enables discounts; easier to reduce than raise prices	8.4
	Small Price Changes	2 percent price change = 20 percent profit change	8.4
	Shop Rate in Job Shop	Methods and mechanics	8.5
	Good, Better, Best	Easy choices; upgrade; decoy effect	8.6, 7.1
	Value in Use	Price based on sharing the value to customer from his savings, not based on your cost	8.7
	Price Structure	Examples with pros and cons; progress payments; late payment penalty	8.8
	Differentiated Pricing	Examples and situations	8.9
	Promotional Pricing	Examples per objective; lifetime customer value	8.10
	Pricing to Distributors	Reasonable markup; markup vs. margin; channel functions and their cost	8.11

Distributors	Becoming Attractive to Distributors	Product; company; the deal you offer; systems; your own personality	9.1
	Finding Distributors	Terminology; finding candidates; qualifying them	9.2
	Distributor Agreements	Exclusivity and quota; returns, launch incentive, manufacturer approved price (MAP)	9.2
Sales	Insight Selling	Types of target companies; "insight" approach; internal allies; sales approach	9.3
	Sales Compensation	Target compensation; salary vs. commission; bonus; promotions (SPIFF)	9.4
	Segmented Compensation	Different incentives for stars, core performers, and laggards	9.5
	Sales Support	Five "helpers" and nine "tools"	9.6
Market Communications	Market Communications (Marcom) Planning	Target audience; different tools for different goals; budgeting techniques	10.1
	Traditional Media	Choose the media that fits the communications task	10.2
	Website Design	Site planning; page planning; content writing; professional designer; updating	10.3
	Using Social Media	Sequence of social media; content selection and calendar	10.4
	Customer Database Design	Purposes; data to capture; operations data entry process	10.5
	Customer Database Reports and Record Design	Envision reports; design their content, then design customer data record to fit how reports will use the data	10.6
	Roadmap for Marketing	Summary of marketing articles with graphic	10.7

Chapter 7: Product Strategy

7.1 Product and Service Bundles: Product Strategy

Marketing starts with standing in the customers' shoes: feeling the customers' needs as they feel them and seeing your company as the customer sees you—the customer perspective.

Product Strategy: Bundled Solutions

When your customer looks at your company, does he see a laundry list of services and products or a few product or service bundles to choose from? If he sees a laundry list, you have expressed what you can do from *your* perspective, not the customer's perspective. Rather than a long list of offerings, you want to anticipate the customer's needs: offer bundles, i.e. *packages of services or options*, planned to meet the most common sets of needs.

When creating these bundles, you realize some customers want more services and more customization than others, yet they do not want to buy more services than they need. Customers appreciate choice, but they also appreciate simplicity. They avoid complexity. So give them a few choices but not too many.

There are two ideas here. One is offering different solutions tailored to different customer situations or needs. The second is packaging groups of services to enable convenient choice. Some want the premium offer, some want a standard set of services, and others want only the basics.

Product Tiers: Good, Better, Best

This second idea is called "product tiers" or levels. As an example, think about buying a new car. The manufacturer offers a long laundry list of options, but he packages them into groups: EX may be basic, LX may be the middle ground, and SX may be the premium package. In an Olympic year, you might think of them like the three Olympic medals: bronze, silver and gold. You choose one package for a single price and then maybe add one or two other "a la carte" options for a separate, additional fee to customize the product to meet your needs.

For example, a photographer may offer wedding photos, graduation photos, family portraits, event photos, and videos for all these as well. In each of these situations, there may be multiple photo sessions, different photo and video editing options, and a variety of media options, from proofs to albums to discs. This is the laundry list. How does he or she structure the website or brochure to simplify the complexity?

Presenting Product Tiers on the Website

The home page might list the types of situations matching the most common customer needs: wedding, graduation, family portrait, and events, with a link to a page for each.

On each "customer situation" page, he offers three product tiers: basic, standard, and premium, using "catchier" names. He presents the tiers in a table, with a column for each level of package (tier) and a column on the left for services. There is a row for each type of service: sessions, proofs, editing, and delivery format. Under each of the tier headings, he enters either an X (if it is provided), or a number (e.g., number of proofs), or types of editing services available in this tier, or leaves it blank if that service is not available in this tier. At the bottom, he provides a link to an "a la carte" services page, where the customer can add a specific service for a specific fee.

This "a la carte services" page can be set up as a table as well, with a row for each service showing the name, a brief description, the standalone price, and a column for "included in package." This entry in this last column would show the name of the packages or tiers that include this service in the package price. For an example, see *Web Hosting | Secure Hosting Plans with Unlimited Bandwidth*.[21]

Customers can go to the page that matches their situation, select the package that fits their need and price range, and then go to the "services" page to add customization. They have a choice, and the choice is simple, yet it can be tailored.

Result: Higher Sales

Customers often decide to upgrade to a package with more services when those who thought they wanted only basic services can easily see what they are missing. Product tiering thus becomes a sales tool!

For more on this product/pricing tool, and a description of how this "decoy effect" leads most to choose a higher level bundle, see Article 8.6.

7.2 Service Design and Positioning

Service Design is not quite the same as designing a physical product. If your product strategy involves designing a service, you must design the *customer experience* to fit with your *positioning*.

Step One: Elements of the Experience

Start by listing each step of the customer's encounter with your service. For example:

1. Become aware the service exists

2. Research providers

3. Buy, order, register

4. Arrive, welcome

5. Receive service

6. Depart

7. Follow up

Step Two: Your Differentiation and Positioning

Earlier you researched customer preferences and how well the competitors meet them and selected your special competitive edge—your *differentiation*. See Article 3.1. *If you are not different—better—than your competitors on something that matters to customers when they are deciding to buy, there is no reason for your business to exist!*

Then you created a benefits-focused way to express how you are better—your positioning. This is a marketing statement that you want prospects to think of when they think of you. Pepsi's differentiation was sweetness. Young people prefer sweeter drinks. So they chose "the Pepsi Generation" as their positioning. They pictured young people having fun while drinking Pepsi; everyone wants to identify with young people having fun!

Maybe you are offering financial management advice. Competitors make it seem complicated, so you choose positioning based on simplicity—everyone wants some simple techniques to manage their finances.

Step Three: Designing the Experience

Design your service by designing the customer's experience. The key concept is this: support that "simple" positioning in every step of the customer's experience.

- For awareness, make sure your website appears when they "Google" *simple* financial management.

- When they do their research, make sure your website and your brochures offer a *simpler* structure than competitors, with tables, clearly labeled techniques, and a step-by-step process.

* When they are ready to sign up for your seminar, *make it easy.* Don't ask for too much information, and provide a way for them to talk to someone to see if the seminar will fit their needs.

* Make sure directions to the site are *clear.*

* When they arrive, the signage should be *clear.* Someone should welcome them in a way that *calms any fears* and encourages questions.

* Delivery of the service—the seminar itself—should stress *simple techniques,* offer easy-to-follow materials, and simple "next steps," such as personal counseling and instructional materials. The overall message fits your positioning: "everyone can do this."

* When the seminar is over, they should leave with a *clear* idea of what to do next, some *simple takeaway materials,* and a *clear* mission for their next steps. Thank them for coming and promise to be *available to help.*

* Then follow up quickly and once more a little later on, with a message of interest and *assistance.*

Designing every step of your service to support your positioning communicates your "edge" through every element of the customer's experience with you. Words are a start, but the experience is crucial to make the words come true!

7.3 Product Roadmap

A Product Roadmap is a plan to develop identified new products or services for introduction at a specific future date. It addresses a major risk in new product strategy—the company may waste time, effort, and money chasing technology upgrades while losing sight of why customers buy.

A Product Roadmap minimizes risk by providing a *disciplined approach to new product development,* based on market needs and competitive advantage. The Roadmap also serves as a communications tool, *aligning employee efforts* toward a common goal, rather than competing for internal resources to develop everyone's favorite idea.

Why New Products?

The most successful businesses earn almost half their revenue from new products—those introduced in the past five years.[22] Businesses refresh their product lines at regular intervals for several reasons:

- To improve their differentiation from competitors or narrow a competitor's differentiation. See Article 3.1.

- To replace revenues as current products enter the later stages of their product life cycle

- To take advantage of new technical developments

- To keep up with evolving market needs or appeal to a new target market segment

The challenge is deciding which new products to introduce when, and gaining commitment to that plan throughout the company. The Product Roadmap technique enables a coherent market-based approach for the next several new products.

Creating the Framework for the Product Roadmap

Design your Roadmap for customer needs, not engineers. Resist the temptation to select new products according to the availability of new technology.

The first step in developing a Product Roadmap is to select the target launch dates. For example, a consumer technology company may decide to launch a major new product around October 1 every year, because 40 percent of consumer electronics are bought in the Christmas season. Then it may decide to launch a minor product update six months earlier every year, around April 1. These intervals are similar to a software version release schedule.

The second step is to decide which market segment to address at each launch date. For example, the company may want to strengthen its competitive position with students or business professionals.

The third step is to decide which of the target market's "buying criteria" to satisfy better. In this decision, the Competitive Analysis Matrix (see Article 3.2) is crucial. This tool reveals how well your company meets the needs of these customers today vs. how well they are met by competitors. Here is where you decide how to improve your competitive edge.

Selecting the New Product Concepts

Once this framework is in place, you decide what kind of improvement is needed for that time, that customer group, and that particular buying criteria.

Anticipate the Price Impact on Your Product Line

Select a price point for the new product, and plan how the prices for your other (existing) products will be modified when the new product is launched.

For example, in early 2010, the Product Roadmap for Amazon's Kindle e-reader might have looked like this:

1. Target Launch	10-1-2010	4-1-2011	10-1-2011
2. Market Segment	Avid readers	Children	Teens and younger adults
3. Buying Criteria	Ease of Use	Lower price	Functionality beyond reading
4. Improvement Needed	Size, battery, memory, display	Other revenue source; control cost	Multimedia; control cost
5. Solution	Better technology	Ad-supported; Wi-Fi only	LCD screen; browser; no camera; touch-screen tablet
6. Price Strategy	No higher than Kindle2, lower for Wi-Fi-only version	Under $100	Higher than Kindle3, substantially < iPad

Once the Roadmap is set, product developers can focus on the technology and packaging, while marketers focus on what content will be available, pricing details, communications, and distribution.

Companies using a Product Roadmap meet market needs with a string of successful launches, and develop a reputation for excellence in innovation and sustainable revenue growth. Above all, they are seen to be well-managed market leaders. These are enviable payoffs! The key is a disciplined approach to product development based on meeting customer needs, rather than simply chasing technology.

Chapter 8: Pricing

8.1 Summary of Ten Pricing Techniques

This article sums up the next ten articles on pricing techniques.

Pricing Basics: Value Positioning and Margin: These are the two basics in pricing. Customers buy value, so you must know what your customers value and how well you deliver that value compared to competitors. Be better and charge more. Margin is price minus production and sales costs. You use margin to pay for your fixed costs and to reach your target profit. So know your costs to set your price, but set it to earn the target profit, not just cover costs.

Margin Analysis Drives Pricing: Understand the cost elements for each product, expressed as a percentage of its sales price. Then you can tinker:

- Change how you use a cost element to reduce its percentage of price.

- Raise the price itself, perhaps in small bites, or only for products facing less competition.

- Bundle low- and high-margin products into a package whose price yields a higher margin overall.

- Stop serving customers who demand low margins.

Pricing Tips: Start High; Big Results from Small Changes: The list price is an umbrella. It allows room underneath for temporary promotions but only if the list price is high enough so that margin remains even after the discount. The other idea is this: small price changes can make a huge percentage change in your bottom line. Customers ignore small changes, but if you understand your margins, you realize that a 10 percent price change could mean a 100 percent change in profits.

Pricing in a Job Shop: Setting the Shop Rate: Avoid the two biggest mistakes—forgetting to include your target profit as one of the "costs" your price must recover, and assuming all paid hours are also billable hours. The tip about small changes having big results applies here, too!

Pricing Technique: Good, Better, Best: Offer customers three levels of quality/service for three different prices. Customers like choice and tend to buy more than the basic tier. Plus, three tiers shows a clear upgrade path to the risk-averse.

Pricing Technique: Value in Use: Set your price according to how much your product saves the customers vs. their alternative. If you save him ten, charge him five. Split the value with him. He's thinking about his value, not your costs, so set your price based on what he is thinking about.

Price Structure Alternatives: What are you charging for? Is it hours, a finished project, a product unit or set, the right to buy some (membership fee), or a right to use (subscription fee)? This article offers nine price structures with pros and cons for each, plus a few recommendations.

Differentiated Prices: Who would happily pay more and who would buy elsewhere for a lower price? You can charge different prices per customer group (e.g., students), per location (e.g., resort), or by time (e.g., due date or show time). This article offers six bases for differentiation and situations for each.

Promotional Pricing: Temporary discount programs can boost sales. The new customers may stay with you for years: what is their lifetime value (profit) to your company? This article explains eight promotion types, but there are many more. Always test your promotion to see if the results are what you expect and are worth the discount.

Pricing to Distributors: What Is a Reasonable Markup? If the producer *margin* is only 15 percent, why does it make sense to expect a wholesaler *markup* of 20 percent and a retailer *markup* of 40 percent? *Margin* and *markup* are not the same thing. Wholesalers and retailers cover their costs out of their markup. As a producer, you must understand the retail price for your product and the costs/value of your distributors. Your product's value vs. competition sets this ceiling, and all the markups and margins work within the range of market price and producer cost.

8.2 Pricing Basics: Value Positioning and Margin

The price you choose for your products is one of the strongest messages you can send. To use it well, you must decide both your *value positioning* and the *minimum margin* you need to meet your goals, *before* deciding your price.

Value Positioning

Positioning means "how the customer thinks of your company"— a mental image or identity that expresses your competitive edge, the benefit you offer. Your company offers some unique benefit that your target customers appreciate, one they prefer to get from you rather than other sources. Otherwise, you should not be in business! See Article 3.1.

This benefit has value, which should be reflected in your price. If you offer more value, your price should be higher. For example, if your device seldom fails and you have the fastest repair turnaround time, you can charge more than a competitor whose unit fails more often or who takes weeks to repair/replace a failed unit.

People do not always buy the lowest-price alternative. People buy value—the best combination of features/functions and price.

* They buy luxury cars, not just Chevys.

* They buy bottled water, even though tap water is free.

* They buy cable TV, even though national networks are free.

* They buy their favorite brand, even though it costs more.

Why? Because that brand meets their needs best within their price range. Their needs include more than raw functionality. The brand they choose will also meet their needs for style and social acceptance, as well as their need to be sure the product will work as advertised, among others.

When setting a price, know what your customers value and how you deliver that value better than competitors. Then set your price higher than those who deliver less value. If your offering has value, your pricing should communicate that. Having the lowest price merely communicates adequacy, not value.

Calculating Minimum Margin

Margin is the difference between the price you charge and your variable cost of production. Your price must provide enough margin to cover:

* variable costs (e.g., labor, materials),

* fixed costs (e.g., rent, insurance), and

* target profit.

The important point is to set the price high enough to recover more than the variable costs to make and deliver the product.

You must collect enough to pay for overhead (fixed costs) and provide the target profit as well.

So you must know what your costs are before setting your price, and you must select a *target profit*, expressed as a *percentage of revenue.*

For example, if you want a 15 percent profit before tax and your fixed costs are 30 percent of revenue, then your variable costs can be as much as 55 percent of revenue (100% − 15% − 30% = 55%). If variable costs are only 45 percent of revenue, then your profit is 25 percent, given fixed costs of 30 percent (100% − 45% − 30% = 25%).

The basic formula is target revenue = variable costs/(fixed costs percentage of revenue + target profit percentage of revenue), or variable costs/.45 in the above example. This formula applies for one product or for the company as a whole.

Value positioning and margin are the two basic considerations for pricing. The next few articles explain a number of pricing techniques based on these two concepts, such as margin analysis, shop rate, good/better/best, value-in-use, various price structures, differential pricing, types of promotions, and distributor margins.

8.3 Margin Analysis Drives Pricing

You know your price must deliver enough margin, after *variable costs*, to cover overhead and leave the *target profit* you want. This means that *margin analysis,* i.e., understanding all your variable costs, is crucial to setting your price.

Variable costs are those costs whose amount changes with another sale. They include:

- materials

- labor

- subcontracted services

- shipping

- sales commission

Owners increase their margins, and hence their profits, by reducing these variable costs on a per product basis. For example, if I cut my variable costs from 55 percent of revenue to 50 percent, then my margin grows from 45 to 50 percent.

Margin Analysis by Product and Customer Group

Margin analysis gets beneath the business P&L. It assesses the margin on *each* product and *each* set of customers.

Owners need to know which products have the highest and lowest margins. There may be a role for low-margin products—to attract new customers or fill a hole in the product line. But there may also be opportunities to raise those low margins by product or process redesign, or charging for shipping, or reducing sales commission for such products.

Why pay the same percentage of commission on sales that generate a different percentage margin? You want salespeople to focus on selling high-margin products, and a differentiated commission plan motivates that behavior.

A second technique is raising the price to achieve the desired margin. If it is not making enough money, why are you selling it? Consider using a series of small increases to get the price where it needs to be. See Article 8.4.

A third technique is to boost the prices and margins for products with little competition. For example, once the customer has bought the main item, you will have little competition for accessories and replacement parts. That means these can be priced with very high margins. One example would be a replacement battery for a laptop computer.

A fourth approach uses innovative bundling. In *"Know Your Sales Margins": Business Profit Margins | Entrepreneur.com,* Randy Myers tells of a company who paired high- and low-margin products into an offer that produced a higher-blended margin. He says, "Think fast-food value meals."[23]

Other examples of pairing high- and low-margin products would be maintenance contracts or a discount on an already-high list price for replacement parts.

The other direction for margin analysis is looking at customer groups. Some types of customers cost more than others. Reasons may include their need for after-sales support, warranty replacements, a lengthy sales cycle, or custom ingredients or processing.

Managing your margins means controlling these extra costs, charging more to cover them, or even "firing" these customers.

Profitability depends on knowing your margins by product and by customer group. Armed with that knowledge, business owners can focus on which costs to control and choose prices that deliver their target margin and profit.

8.4 Pricing Tips: Start High; Big Results from Small Changes

For a new business or new product, the pricing mantra is "Start High." For a business already in operation, you must understand the effect of a small price increase on your profit level.

Start High

"Start high" makes sense for these reasons:

* **List price communicates the product's value vs. competing products.** If you price low, you are sending the message that your value is less than the competitor's. See Article 8.2.

* **Pricing is a game with several moves,** including the competitor's responses and your discounts. If you try to become the low-price alternative, you will find the competitors matching you. Then what is your competitive edge? If you reduce your price further, the competitors will also match your price. Then you are in a price war, which you will lose quickly if your price starts out low. You will not have enough margin to cover costs and meet target profit goals.

* **The list price is an umbrella,** providing room for temporary promotions designed for a temporary boost in sales and hence revenue. A high list price provides enough profit margin to allow for special-purpose discounts and promotions that can still be profitable. If your list price is too low, your *average price* after factoring in discounts/promotions may be too low to meet your profit goals.

- **Price cuts are easier than price increases.** If you find your price is too high for your sales goals, customers will always welcome various discount programs or even a reduced list price. However, if you find your price is too low, increases must be carefully managed to avoid driving customers away.

Small Price Increases

The fastest way to increase revenue is to raise your price, but small business owners value their customers and are afraid that a price increase may drive them away. Fear not—instead, analyze!

- **Small increases can have a major effect on profits.** Assume your price is $20 and your profit after overhead is 10 percent of sales, or $2. A 10 percent increase in price would be $2, raising the price from $20 to $22, but this would double your profit to $4! A 10 percent price increase boosted profits 100 percent.

- **Small increases are accepted by customers who value your offering.** Would you change suppliers for a $2 price bump? It may be 10 percent, but it is still only $2. How many people stopped using the Illinois Tollway when it nearly doubled prices? Not many, because it still offered value vs. slower alternatives. If your product cannot hold customers with a 10 percent price increase, find ways to increase the value customers find in your product (e.g., "open road tolling"), and *then* raise the price!

- **Regular (annual) small price increases have even less impact, because customers learn to expect them.** This is the cable TV strategy. Expected changes are hardly changes at all. With annual increases, the amount can be as low as 2 percent. The best strategy couples regular list price increases with attractive introductory rates and loyalty reward programs. The high list price enables the discounts (which help attract and retain customers) without missing target profit goals.

If you are starting out, "start high." If you are in business, use regular small list-price increases to maintain margins while offering targeted discounts for selective purposes.

8.5 Pricing in a Job Shop: Setting the Shop Rate

A "job shop" sells custom-made parts that are produced according to customer specifications, usually in small quantities. Job shops develop a *price quote* for each job, rather than establishing a standard list price per product.

Their "*shop rate*" is a bundled price applied to *billable labor hours* (those spent on the job being quoted). It is designed to capture enough revenue to cover labor costs, overhead, and target profit. Setting the right "shop rate" is the key to their profitability.

This article provides the techniques for calculating a shop rate. For example, employees may earn $25/hour, but the company may need to charge its customers $75 to $100 per hour spent on a job, to recover overhead and profit as well as labor costs.

Step One: Estimate Costs and Target Profit

First, estimate the costs to be recovered by the shop rate for the coming year. For our example, we assume the following costs are passed through to the customer without markup: materials, subcontractors, shipping. This means the shop rate must recover labor, overhead, profit, and sales commissions.

Labor includes hourly wages (whether or not they are billable on jobs) plus benefits and related payroll taxes. Overhead includes the owner's salary, benefits, and payroll taxes, plus fixed costs, such as rent, utilities, insurance, maintenance, computers, vehicles, depreciation on equipment, etc.

Profit will be a dollar amount, not a percentage of revenue at this point, because revenue is unknown. Assume the profit target is an amount equal to the owner's salary.

Sales commissions might normally be 5 percent of revenue, but we do not know revenue yet. Use one-sixth of salary plus overhead (excluding labor) as an estimate, based on the assumption that salary plus overhead will turn out to be 30 percent of revenue.

For this example, assume the following: owner's salary is $50K, other overhead aside from labor is $100K; profit is $50K, sales commission is $25K, nonbillable labor cost is $80K, and billable labor cost is $120K. *This assumes 60 percent of paid labor time is billable on jobs.* The rest is setup/cleanup, training, paid time off, and miscellaneous. Thus the shop rate must recover $425K.

Step Two: Estimate Annual Billable Hours and Calculate the Shop Rate

Second, estimate the number of billable hours for the year. Billable labor costs of $120K less 10 percent payroll tax and 10 percent benefits leaves approximately $100K. Divide that by $25/hour to get 4,000 billable hours.

The resulting shop rate is $425K/4,000 hours, or $106.25 per hour. This is an illustration, not a recommended price! Your shop rate depends on your own numbers: overhead, salary, profit, wage rate, etc. However, note that it is not unusual for the shop rate to be three or four times the hourly wage rate.

Avoid Two Common Errors

One common error in calculating the shop rate is omitting the target profit. Another is assuming all paid labor hours are also billable hours.

Job shop owners should review their shop rate at least annually. The tip about small changes having big results (see Article 8.4) applies here as well: raising your shop rate by $2 may increase your profits by 20 percent. Use your own numbers and check it out!

8.6 Pricing Technique: Good, Better, Best

Three-tiered pricing is a popular and proven pricing technique. It goes by many names: good, better, best; economy, standard, premium; bronze, silver, gold; consumer, professional, expert, etc. The idea is to give customers a choice and a basis for comparison but not choice overload—not a laundry list. See Article 7.1.

Offer Choice, But Make It Easy to Choose

Buyers appreciate choice. It shows that the seller respects them by responding to a variety of customer requirements and price ranges. Choice also gives buyers a basis for comparison because it shows how the price changes when different features are added or subtracted. As a result, buyers can be comfortable they made a good buying decision because they bought only as much as they needed.

On the other hand, buyers do not respond well to *choice overload*. They expect the seller to anticipate some common sets of needs and design packages to address them. Examples are all around us: software versions, car models, Olympic medals, etc. For some reason, the human brain is comfortable with sets of three. Even jokes often cite three situations, with the third containing the punch line!

Why Three Tiers?

Sellers like three-tier pricing, too. First, it communicates everything they can do without requiring everyone to buy the premium package. Merely defining the premium package communicates the extent of the seller's capabilities, thus earning credibility. Buyers who choose a lower tier still have the comfort that they can upgrade to a higher tier without losing their investment.

Second, three-tier pricing appeals to a wider market. It offers an affordable entry level, as well as the complete package for high-end buyers. Sellers can use the lower tiers to compete against discounters without risking a price war, while showing their capabilities to those willing to spend more to get more.

Third, experience shows that more people choose a higher price alternative when three tiers are offered vs. two! This has been called the "decoy effect." See *"We're All Predictably Irrational,"* *Dan Ariely, YouTube.*[24]

How to Do Three-Tier Pricing

1. Establish three versions of your product, geared to three types of customers or three common sets of customer needs.

2. Find a way (often a table) to show at a glance which services fall into each tier. This enables customers to compare, as well

as to understand the full extent of the seller's capabilities. See Article 7.1.

3. Offer an *upgrade path*. Those who buy a lower tier should be able to see that they can customize by ordering additional services on an *a la carte* basis. This helps customers manage the risk of overbuying or underbuying, which increases their comfort level. However, the *a la carte* price is usually higher than if they bought some predetermined set of services in the higher tier.

For a familiar example, think about buying a new car. Auto manufacturers offer three sets of features, packaging the options into manageable sets with three progressive price levels. If you want to add a feature a la carte, you can do so, but may have to wait for it to be built that way. To get your car right away, you can buy the higher feature set or save a little by foregoing the desired feature and buying a lower-level package or model.

8.7 Pricing Technique: Value in Use

"Value in use" pricing means the price is based on the product's value to the customer, not the manufacturer's cost of production. For example, if a normal saw blade is priced at $7 and you create one that lasts four times as long, the *value to the customer* of the long-life blade would be $28, aside from saving the time involved in changing blades. What price should you set for the long-life blade?

Assuming the blade-changing effort is minimal, you will want to set your price below $28, since that is the point where the customer is indifferent to one of your new blades vs. four of the old blades. A price level somewhere between $14 and $21 seems reasonable if there is no competition for your new blade. If you price it at $17, the buyer and the seller each take half the increase in value. The difference is large enough to get the buyer's attention and make him consider changing his habitual purchase behavior.

Using $17 as a test price level, you can then consider your development costs and any production cost difference between the old and the new blade, to see the effect of this price level on your margins. The price you choose should be low enough that customers see significant value but high enough to generate premium margins while leaving room for price cuts when competitors match your innovation.

Obviously, this is not "*cost-based pricing*," and it is not "*pricing to competition*." The price is based on the value to the customer who buys the long-life blade. Only after establishing that value do you consider your cost and potential competitive responses.

Provide an Upgrade Path

Many customers will quickly understand the higher value of the higher-priced long-life blade. But some may not need this value yet. To widen the market, consider an *upgrade path* for those not yet ready to change.

To illustrate, we need to change our example. Consider a server equipped with new software, enabling it to work so fast that it can do the work of four servers. You want to set prices for three customer groups:

1. *Data-Hogs*: buyers who need to buy more than two servers

2. *Entrants*: those who think they need to buy only one or two servers

3. *Upgraders*: those who already own one server, then realize the need to add one or more new servers

Assume the old server price is $10,000, and you decide to price the new hardware/software package at $20,000. This is a great deal for *data-hogs* and delivers high margin for the seller. Smaller data users, the other two segments, are attractive for their numbers and future growth, but $20,000 is a much higher price than your competitor offers for an old-style server adequate for their current needs.

The solution is to continue to offer your old server at $10,000, like the competition, but enhance its value vs. the competition by offering to equip it with the new four-times-faster software when the customer is ready. This is an upgrade path.

How would you price this software-only retrofit? The upgrade price should be more than $10,000, to avoid competing with your new server priced at $20,000. It should be less than $20,000, because otherwise the customer, who already has one server, could just buy two more old servers from you or your competitor and see no price difference. A reasonable price for the software-only upgrade would be 1.5 times the price of an old server: $15,000.

This table summarizes a "value in use" pricing plan for this example:

Customer Need	1 Server	2 Servers	3 Servers	4 Servers
Today's Customer Spends	10,000	20,000	30,000	40,000
New *Data-Hog* spends $20K: HW/SW package	20,000	20,000	20,000	20,000
Entrant spends $10-$25K: HW + retrofit	10,000	15,000		
Upgrader spends $15K: SW-only retrofit		15,000	15,000	15,000

Those who buy the package pay $20,000, while those who buy in two steps pay $25,000. Yet previous customers get the new technology for $5,000 less than new buyers, recognizing the value of the current customer base.

Offering the choice of a software-only upgrade sets a value for the software. Here is a side benefit. The *retrofit choice* actually defines the value of the *package offer* as a better deal: new hardware for half the old hardware price, plus growth at no cost.

By offering the upgrade as an alternative to the package offer, the seller is actually enhancing the perception of the package offer's value. This is a good example of the "decoy effect" that results from offering different alternatives, cited in Article 8.6.

8.8 Price Structure Alternatives

Your "price structure" is what you charge for (product or service component or package) and when the payment is due. For example, you might charge an hourly rate or a package price for an entire job.

Your price structure should meet some or all of these goals:

* more margin per unit sold

* sell more units

* obtain cash flow early enough to enable continued operations

* ensure on-time payments

* reduce customer resistance for reasons of credibility or fear of exceeding budget

* reduce your risk of costs exceeding budget

Some common price structure alternatives used in different industries:

Technique/Example	Seller Pro/Con	Buyer Pro/Con
Per Package, Not Per Unit — Package of Wood Screws	*Pro:* Sell more units *Con:* May need to discount the package price (e.g., price for package of 50 = price for 35 units bought individually)	*Pro:* Simplicity *Con:* Am I paying for more screws than I need?
Per Deal, Not Per Hour — Consultant	*Pro:* Customer has certainty *Con:* Risk of poor estimate requires raising estimated hrs. by 10-20% to get basis for package price	*Pro:* Certainty for budget *Con:* Am I paying for more hours than I am getting?
Per Hour, Not to Exceed X without Customer OK — Consultant	*Pro:* Customer has control *Con:* No risk of underestimating	*Pro:* Control for budget *Con:* Control is imperfect; when consultant asks for OK to exceed, I will need to grant it for project to be completed

Retainer Plus Price of Excess Units – Lawyer	Pro: Covers setup time/cost; provides opportunity to develop relationship and prove value; customer decision at a lower price point makes it easier for him to say yes	Pro: Smaller purchase before relationship is developed
		Con: No upper limit means lack of control, but customer can always say stop!
	Con: Customer who would have paid high package price objects to "nickel and diming"	
Base Product Price, Plus Price for Additional Options – Car	Pro: Simplicity in product package; sell more options than if they were ordered individually	Pro: Simplicity of package
		Con: Buy more options than needed
List Price Less Various Discounts – Insurance	Pro: Discounted price makes customer feel good; manages price level to risk level	Pro: Discounts make customer feel like a wise shopper
	Con: Company may appear high-priced if only list prices are compared	Con: Availability and amount of discounts not clear at outset
"Progress Payments" through the Course of the Work – Construction	Pro: Match timing of cash received to timing of expenses paid	Pro: Spread out payments
		Con: Cash is paid out before value is received
	Con: Customer may resist paying before results received	
Discount for Payment within 30 Days	Pro: Motivates timely payment	Pro: Discounts always welcome
	Con: Some clients pay late and take the discount anyway!	Con: May wish to pay later
Late Payment Penalty for Payment after Due Date	Pro: Motivates timely payment; avoids late payers taking a discount as above	Pro: None
		Con: Pressure to pay
	Con: Collecting is difficult, but message is sent even without collecting	

Recommended techniques are:

* Consultant price per hour up to a maximum, requiring client approval to exceed it (balances risk of error in forecast, for both buyer and seller)

* Base price for package of features, plus "a la carte" charge for options

* Progress payments: these can be crucial to keeping your business solvent!

* Late payment penalty: avoids clients paying late but taking a discount anyway

8.9 Differentiated Pricing

"Differentiated Pricing" means different prices for the same product in different situations. Familiar examples are senior discounts, high prices at airports and resorts, and lower prices for last-minute tickets.

The goal of differentiated pricing is to earn higher margins in one of two ways:

* higher prices in a location with less competition (airport, resort, pro shop, entertainment venue)

* lower prices whose lower margins are offset by producing enough additional sales to gain higher profits overall (last-minute sales of vacant rooms or cheap tickets)

For the small business owner, the challenge is to *know the market* well enough to be sure the differentiated price really does generate higher margins. Will that senior discount really draw more customers? At a movie theater, if popcorn costs less, how many more buckets would be sold?

Test It!

Like most other marketing initiatives, the best way to find out is to *test*. Try a differentiated price, publicize it, and see how many sales result. Ideally, you would also ask customers if they would have bought anyway at the old price.

A very common error in putting this "test it" advice into practice is failure to publicize: "we tried that for a week and got no uplift," or "no, we didn't change our marketing—that would have cost too much." Do not test if you will not be telling customers about it!

Another common error is hit-and-miss recordkeeping about test results: "our afternoon clerk didn't know he or she was supposed to tally or ask or offer…"

Common Price Differentiation Techniques

Basis for Differentiation	Situations with Special Prices
Customer Segment	Discounts for students; seniors; residents of taxing (e.g., park) district
Product Form	Ascending price per milligram for sweetener box vs. packets vs. tablets
Channel of Distribution	Ascending price for online vs. big box store vs. specialty store
Location	Higher price for spot with less competition (pro shop, airport, resort); lower price in outlet center
Time	Lower price for advance purchase; lowest price for last-minute purchase of perishable goods (the highest cost hotel room to the hotelier is the empty one)
Geography	Ascending golf fees for rural vs. urban vs. resort; lower-cost plane ticket when flying from a low-income country

8.10 Promotional Pricing

Promotions are temporary. *Promotional pricing* is designed to provide a temporary boost in sales, by offering more attractive terms than the standard list price and options.

Unlike differentiated prices (see Article 8.9), promotional prices are available to all buyers, with the possible exception of a credit check for a promotion involving better credit terms. But the same question applies to both promotional and differentiated prices: are the additional sales worth more than the reduced margin per sale?

To answer this key question, companies always *test* their promotion. They introduce it for a narrow slice of the market or products, publicize it, track the additional sales, and assess whether any profit improvement resulted from the discount.

When testing, the same cautions apply: be sure to publicize the promotion; be sure to track it fully, and try to determine whether the customer would have bought anyway at the original price.

Types of Promotions

There may be as many types of promotions as there are stars in the sky! Owners design promotions according to market demand and product profitability, and the only limit is their creativity. Some examples are:

Promotion Type	Definition	Objective
Buy One Get One Free (BOGO)	Two for price of one	Increase unit sales; useful when production cost is a small percentage of total cost
Loss Leader	Price below cost	Attract new buyers to the product line; sell more high-margin accessories or tie-ins
Special Event Pricing	Limited time sale price	Attract more buyers now who will return later and/or buy accessories or tie-ins
Cash rebate	Sell for list price but offer discount via cash back	Maintain list price; offer appearance of a deal; reduce cost of discount by percentage of buyers who do not pursue the rebate procedure
Low-Interest Financing	As stated	Maintain list price; attract more buyers via lower monthly payment; seller pays part of interest cost
Longer Payment Terms or No Payments Until (Delayed Start)	As stated	Maintain list price; attract more buyers via lower monthly payment; seller may borrow working capital to replace delayed cash flow
Longer Warranty	As stated	Maintain list price; attract more buyers by reducing their perceived risk; useful when most warranty issues occur early in the product's life
Free Component (Free Razor; Pay for Blades)	As stated	Attract more buyers; useful when most margins result from sale of consumable accessory (blades)

Promotion Cost vs. Lifetime Value

Promotions make financial sense when you consider the *lifetime value of the customer* to your business. It is worth incurring a cost (lower margin) to gain a customer who will make subsequent purchases that generate high margins. Examples are automobile servicing, blades for razors, e-book purchases vs. e-reader device, credit card interest, replacement parts, etc.

To do the math, you need to consider the cost and the gains. Costs include lost margin for those who would have bought anyway (eventually) and publicity costs. Gains include any margin on the original sale from those who would *not* have bought from you, plus the margin from their subsequent purchases, for as long as they buy from you.

How long does your average customer buy from you? For example, one credit card issuer calculated an average customer life of eight years. This issuer chooses promotions to gain new customers where cost of the promotion (such as a lower interest rate for the first year) is less than the total margins they earn from those new customers over the next seven years.

Do the math, run the test, redo the math after seeing results of the test, then launch the promotion or modify the offer, and test again.

8.11 Pricing to Distributors: What Is a Reasonable Markup?

Distributors are the middle component of a *three-tier distribution* chain: producer to distributor to retailer. The distributor is the "middleman." The distributor and the retailer incur their own costs in bringing the product to customers, and both need to recover those costs and earn adequate margins.

In setting their price to distributors, producers must understand both distributor and retailer functions and costs. Producers must also understand the ceiling on their product's retail price level as dictated by product value and competitive alternatives.

For example, imagine a product priced at $100 retail. Potential pricing for a three-tier distribution model might be:

	Cost	Markup	Selling Price
Manufacturer	$51.77	15%	$59.53
Wholesaler	$59.53	20%	$71.43
Retailer	$71.43	40%	$100

In this example, the manufacturer's price to the wholesaler is 59.5 percent of the retail price. Let's assume that the manufacturer's cost includes an allocation of all his overhead, so his 15 percent markup is pure profit. The total markup by all three players is $48.33, or 92 percent of the manufacturer's cost.

To allow "room" for markups by downstream players, the manufacturer must know the likely retail price. This is determined not by retailer whim but by value to users relative to competition and their prices. See Article 8.7.

Wholesaler markups average 20 percent and will not exceed 30 to 40 percent, according to *"The Average Profit Margin for Wholesale"* | *Small Business, Chron.com.*[25]

For the retailer markup over what he pays the wholesaler, situations vary depending on the size and market power of the players, but a typical *retailer markup* would be at least 40 percent for big box retailers and more for boutiques. In this example, the difference is 40 percent: (100 – 71.43 = 28.57) / 71.43 = .40.

Markup Is Not the Same as Margin!

In the example above, the retailer marked up the price 40 percent, but his margin was 28.57 percent. For markup, you divide profit by cost. For margin, you divide profit by price. See *"Pricing, Markup, Margins and Mass Confusion"* | *Brooding on Matters* | *Travis T.*[26]

Channel Margins Tool by Harvard Business School Publishing[27] provides a handy online calculator for markup and margin in a four-tier distribution model.

Channel Functions Create Their Costs

The wholesaler's price to the retailer determines not only the wholesaler's markup; it also becomes the base for the retailer's markup. Competition defines the retail price ceiling, so the retailer's markup will be that market-determined retail price minus the wholesaler's price. To understand what markup is fair for both players, you first must understand what value they are adding and their related costs.

Wholesaler Functions	Retailer Functions
Buying the Product	Buying the Product
Promoting/Contracting with Retailers to Sell It	Promoting/Contracting with Consumers to Buy It
Inventory Risks and Facility Costs	Inventory Risks and Store Costs
Assembling Product Assortments	In-Store Merchandising
Sorting: Break Down into Small Quantities	Shelving
Delivery to Retailers	Delivery to Customers
Financing Retailer Buys	Financing Customer Buys
Grading the Product	Handling Returns
Market Info Feedback to Manufacturer	Market Feedback to Wholesaler

Retailers have higher costs than wholesalers for their facility and for their advertising, promotions, and merchandising, while wholesalers have higher delivery costs than retailers.

In general, retailers have higher costs than wholesalers to perform their functions. This means retailers need a higher percentage markup between what they pay to buy the product and what they can sell it for. This markup is mostly used to cover their costs. Only a small percentage remains as a margin for their business.

Alternative: Cut Out the Middleman

At this point one or two players in the chain start to think about *vertical integration*. For example, the manufacturer considers whether he can deal with retailers himself to save the wholesaler's markup.

But here is a "word to the wise": in doing so, you will have to perform the wholesaler's functions yourself, so at best you would save the wholesaler's margin, not the entire markup, most of which goes to covering his costs which you would then incur.

For an example of comparing channel costs, see *"Understanding the Economics of Your Product Distribution Channels"* : *Money.*[28]

Chapter 9: Distributors and Sales Force

9.1 Attracting Distributors to Reach Retailers

Every retailer dreams of a constant flow of new products, and so do the distributors they depend on. But distributing a new product from a new business introduces some risk. Can distributors depend on production and quality? Will the new product get enough promotion to take off? Can the start-up pay for its marketing costs?

Before you start your search for distributors, take some time to make your business attractive to them. Finding someone who will "just say no" is a waste. First, make yourself ready, and then begin the hunt!

Becoming Attractive

Becoming attractive to distributors has five dimensions: your product, your company, the deal you offer, your systems, and you yourself as a client and colleague.

1. Product Attractiveness: The distributor knows the market and quickly assesses your product. He's looking for a product with an easily understood value and differentiation, high sales volume from repeat purchases, enough variety to attract a wide set of users, and a price level that fits the retailers he serves. Standout packaging helps as well.

Is this you? Can you provide some evidence of your product's popularity, such as a survey or test market or focus group results?

2. Company Attractiveness: If the product is attractive, the distributor begins to consider your company. Do you have a solid plan to support the product, and will you be able to sustain that program? The question is credibility. He is looking for a business plan that shows a strong marketing program, quality production process, and financial strength to support marketing and production.

The distributor is especially interested in marketing communications, such as

- product name
- tag line (positioning)
- sales promotions

- spokespersons
- demos, samples, point of sales materials
- social media program
- public relations plan

He is looking for "pull" from potential customers. If you can create pull or you have a plan to support distributors and retailers in their efforts to create pull, then he will have a reason to supply more and more to his retailers.

What are you doing to create pull? Do you have references to help make your plan believable?

3. Deal Attractiveness: Your deal with the distributor involves the services he provides for you, the support you provide for him, and his compensation.

If the distributor is really just a wholesaler, one who merely delivers product to his retailer customers, his fee is small. If he delivers and does merchandising as well, making attractive store displays that set your product apart from the competition, his fee is higher.

If he buys the product from you, his markup must allow for the retailer's markup as well as his own services, and you will need a three-tier pricing plan: price paid by distributor, price paid by retailer, price paid by customer. In addition, you must be prepared to buy ads in trade publications, put your product in the distributor's mailer or catalog, and train his people.

Distributor markups start at 20 percent and increase depending on the services they provide. Retailer markup might be 40 percent. If you sell to the distributor at $100, he sells to the retailer at a minimum of $120 and the retailer sells to the public at a minimum of $168. See Article 8.11.

Is your deal attractive? For more on deal terms, see the next article.

4. Systems Attractiveness: Systems is all about "ease of doing business" with you. The distributor prefers:

* automated 24/7 interfaces for orders, shipping status, product delivery, funds due and funds paid, leads, and product changes

* sales support tools such as product information, benefits, and answers to common objections

While he wants to be able to contact you personally whenever he needs to, he prefers products where there is no need to talk to the producer in the normal course of business. This may not be a deal-breaker at the outset, but its absence can cause deals to fall apart later.

Do you have a plan for a distributor platform or portal?

5. Your Attractiveness: Distributors will take the time to learn the attractiveness of your product and your business if they enjoy talking to you. Their sales and merchandising efforts will be affected by your relationship of mutual respect and support. If that is missing, the distributor's effort will be missing, too.

How Can Your Business Help the Distributor?

Becoming attractive to a business colleague is only a little about *your own* prospects for success. It is mostly about *his* success.

It starts with your respect for the distributor's business and knowledge and your willingness to make his important job easier by doing everything you can to support his efforts.

You must know enough to know what you must do to help: the basics and something extra. Then he will pay attention to your attractive product and company so a deal may be made.

You can differentiate your business by differentiating yourself as a person who is "easy to do business with."

Now that your attractiveness is assured, the next article addresses finding the right distributor!

9.2 Finding the Right Distributor

You are a small company with a new product, and you need to find the right distributor(s) to place your product on retailer shelves and help promote it. Finding the right distributor is a four-step process: understand the industry's distribution channels, develop a list of candidate distributors, qualify the candidates, and finally agree on a distribution deal.

Finding the Right Distributor

Every industry has its own unique distribution channel structure. To understand yours, research trade association magazines and attend trade shows to talk to distributors and retailers. But first, understand the terminology.

* You want a distributor who will *buy the product* from you, not just take orders and deliver. You want him to own the inventory and collect from retailers. This is often called a "wholesaler" function, and it is part of being a distributor.

For example, a regional wholesaler buys large lots, takes delivery, breaks them down, and sells smaller lots to local wholesalers or directly to retailers.

* Your distributor should *help sell the product*, not just deliver it. After all, he knows the retailers; you do not. The key word here is "merchandising"—placing the product and related displays within the retailer's space in ways that enhance sales. Examples: end-of-aisle display, brand testing or demo/sample days, brochure placement.

  Sales help is what makes a distributor different than a wholesaler, but some people use the words interchangeably, so be sure to verify whether merchandising is part of what they are talking about.

Expect to pay more for more services: wholesalers who do not provide merchandising are cheaper than distributors. But be aware: saving on distributor expenses can reduce total revenue and profit.

Make a List of Candidates

The second step is to make a list of candidate distributors. Criteria would be: do they serve your industry, will they buy the product for resale, will they do merchandising, and do they already serve the main retailers you want?

Find candidates by asking your target retailers for the name of the distributor who services them for your category of product. Several other sources are:

* Exhibitor's list from trade shows in your industry. See *www.tsnn.com* for a list of trade shows.[29]

* Trade magazines and trade associations. Distributors are always members and often advertise in industry publications. Some sources include the magazine *Modern Distribution Management,* the National Association of Wholesaler-Distributors (NAW), *www.TradePub.com*, and websites like *www.ezGoo.com*.[30]

* For lists of trade associations, see Gale's Encyclopedia of Associations. There is also an American Society of Association Executives.[31]

Qualify These Candidates

The third step is to qualify the candidates on your list.

- Do they serve your geography and your target retailers?

- Are you large enough to matter to them?

- Are they available, or do they already have an exclusivity agreement with a competitor?

- Will they buy your product for resale?

- Do they perform merchandising?

- Do they require exclusive distribution rights? If so, will they agree to a reasonable sales quota?

- Do they require restrictions on pricing or Internet sales? Will they agree to follow your pricing plan?

How do you find this qualifying information? Check their websites. Ask retailers who use them. Ask candidate distributors for a sample distribution agreement. Finally, meet with them! This will be your best opportunity to see if they meet your criteria and to sell your own attractiveness. See Article 9.1.

Agree on a Deal

Once you have found a distributor who can meet your needs, the remaining issue is whether you can agree on a deal. A few words about key deal elements are appropriate here.

1. If you grant exclusivity for a territory, require a sales quota to be met. If this target is not met, you are free to add another distributor and/or cancel this one, and this one is free to stop selling your product.

2. You will need to provide an acceptable policy/process for returned goods, repairs, and warranty claims. The distributor's retail network needs this to keep its customers happy and coming back.

3. If your product has not launched yet in this distributor's territory, be prepared to offer him a higher discount/lower price for a few months after the launch. This will compensate him for the extra "missionary" work he will be doing to place, announce, and promote your new product.

4. Price is the heart of the deal. The distributor's concern is that the manufacturer's price to him is low enough to enable both other players (distributor and retailer) to make their target profit and still do a good job of promoting sales. In addition to agreement on the three-tier pricing plan,

  – To control excessive markups by distributors, your agreement will have a Manufacturer's Approved Pricing (MAP) clause, where distributors agree to a maximum price they will charge to retailers.

- The MAP may also have rules restricting discounting by retailers, which distributors must monitor. If there are no exception conditions, such as for high-volume retailers, this results in a "fair trade" or constant price to consumers across all retailers. For example, Apple does this.

- The MAP might also have a maximum price retailers may charge to their customers.

When the manufacturer fails to control pricing by the other two players, prices to consumers increase as the other two players seek higher margins. Then sales begin to fall. The manufacturer may then cut out the distributor and go direct to the retailer.

While this makes sense on paper, it results in the manufacturer acting as distributor. Unfortunately, the manufacturer usually lacks the relationships, facilities, and merchandising and collection skills that led him to use a distributor in the first place. The outcome is product failure. The reason is the manufacturer failed to insist on price discipline in the distributor agreement. So don't be that guy!

9.3 Insight Sales Replaces Solution Selling

Solution selling was the innovation of the 1980s. Most B2B salespeople operating today were trained to sell solutions—find the need that fits your product, propose a solution, and work with an internal sponsor to gain client agreement.

Recent research shows that the most successful salespeople today have moved beyond solution selling to *insight selling*. The world has changed since the 1980s, and clients no longer rely on the salesperson to invent solutions for recognized needs. Clients now use Internet sources, sophisticated procurement teams, and widely experienced purchasing consultants to define solutions for themselves.

"In fact, a recent Corporate Executive Board study of more than 1,400 B2B customers found that those customers completed, on average, nearly 60 percent of a typical purchasing decision—researching solutions, ranking options, setting requirements, benchmarking pricing, and so on—before even having a conversation with a supplier," according to "The End of Solution Sales," by Brent Adamson, Matthew Dixon, and Nicholas Toman, *Harvard Business Review*, July-August 2012.[32]

The result is price-oriented procurement contests rather than high-margin solution sales.

Insight Selling

The HBR article cited above presents research showing that the star sellers (top 20 percent) have evolved to "insight selling." They seek out customers whose companies are in a state of flux with emerging demands.

These companies are ready to re-examine the status quo. They are receptive to "disruptive ideas" from salespeople who apply their wide experience to the company's situation to identify previously unrecognized needs and suggest new goals and new ways to meet them. By offering change-making insights, these salespeople transform their role from peddler to valuable resource for change.

While solution sellers are trained to work with friendly informants within the company (guides, friends, climbers, together called "talkers"), insight sellers seek out change agents (go-getters, teachers, skeptics, together called "mobilizers") who can move the organization to adopt new ways of looking at the market and new solutions that fit the new perspective.

For insight sellers, the target audience is those who seek outside experts to share insights about what the company should do and who are engaged by big, disruptive ideas. Mobilizers are thinkers. They test the salesperson with tough questions. The conversations are challenging, but the result is a well-customized solution and a well-armed advocate.

Star sellers test the mobilizers in turn, challenging them to bring more information and set up meetings with senior decision-makers. If the mobilizer does not respond, the star seller knows this client is really just a talker and directs his or her efforts elsewhere.

Having found the mobilizer, the final stage requires the seller to *coach the client* through the company's purchasing process. This is a role reversal vs. solution selling, because mobilizers are idea people who are often weak in the political/relationship skills needed for consensus-building. Experienced star sellers are better able to anticipate likely objections and interdepartmental politics than the idea-driven mobilizers. This coaching role is consistent with the salesperson's insight-provider role.

What's Different?

In summary, what makes insight selling different is the:

* **Target company**: in a state of flux; challenged by the need to change status quo; able to decide quickly rather than a company who merely understands its own "established demand."

* **Approach**: offer insights to identify problems and solutions based on broad knowledge rather than merely responding to customer-requested solutions.

* **Target ally**: mobilizers (go-getters, teachers, skeptics) who respond to challenges rather than talkers (guides, friends, climbers).

* **Sales process**: coach the mobilizer through the anticipated purchasing process rather than rely on the "guide" to explain the company's process.

Repeat sales are the payoff for this extra effort and these tough conversations. The authors found that "the biggest driver of B2B customer loyalty is a supplier's ability to deliver new insights."

9.4 Sales Team Compensation Package

When a business owner asks, "how do I pay my salespeople?" at least one question is already settled. He or she has decided to employ a direct sales force rather than (or in addition to) using some type of agent or manufacturer's representative.

He or she has decided the benefits of controlling an exclusive sales force are worth the extra costs and management challenges that might be avoided by using indirect sales. In either approach, the company must provide effective sales support. See Article 9.6.

Much is written about sales force compensation. It is a fascinating saga of the power of incentives and human psychology. However, just asking yourself a few questions can be enough to guide you to an effective plan.

1. How much do you want your average-performing salesperson to earn in a year?

You want to attract good performers, so you must pay a competitive rate. An internet search easily reveals free surveys of sales salaries, and these can become your external benchmark. Then, internally, you must decide what percentage of revenue should be spent on sales salary/benefits and commissions, as part of the profit estimate in your business plan.

For example, if average salespeople need to earn $90,000 (external) and sales costs should be no more than 5 percent of revenue (internal), it will be simple to calculate the number of salespeople you can afford for a particular revenue estimate.

2. How much of those earnings should be salary, based on the kind of results you want?

Different kinds of sales require different levels of time and effort. New accounts and new products are time-consuming sales. When there is a floor on margin-per-sale, more salesperson time and effort is required, because the sale must be made on benefits, not just price. New salespeople need time to build the relationships that must precede the sale.

These more difficult sales goals imply a compensation package where salary is a higher percentage of the total, because commissions will be slower to develop and there is a higher risk of failure due to greater unknowns.

For example, salary might be only 30 percent of average compensation when the product is known by the market, many sales are repeat purchases requiring little sales effort, and the focus is on selling more of the same to a stable customer base. In contrast, salary might rise to 60 to 70 percent of total compensation if the product is struggling for recognition or positioning and every sale is to a new customer.

3. What should be the basis for the commission portion?

Remember the old saying "You get what you measure"? If commission is based on units sold, you will get lots of unit sales but low revenue per sale, as the sales force offers discounts to sell more units to earn more commissions. If the basis is margin, you may get less unit sales but more profits per sale.

Generally, the commission basis is sales revenue with some administrative control over permissible discounts, plus extra "points" or a higher commission percentage when the sale is to a new account.

Also, commissions on new or higher-margin products may earn a higher percentage commission than sales of legacy or lower-margin products. "Win-back" is another differentiated kind of sale that is often paid a higher commission. A "win-back" is an account that had previously switched from your brand to a competitor and now is purchasing your brand again.

For example, the high-margin/new product commission boost might be 10 percent above the normal commission, and the new account boost might be another 10 percent, while the win-back boost might be 15 percent. Note there is potential for collusion and abuse wherever extra commission is paid, including for win-backs.

4. How do you want to compensate above-average performance in a year?

Yes, you *do* want rewards to rise with performance! A ceiling or maximum payout is probably a *bad* idea, as long as the sales and profits growth rate is equal to or better than the commission growth rate.

One approach to reward high performers is an annual bonus calculated as a percentage of commissions earned above the year's target level. Another method is a stepped commission schedule, where successively higher rates are paid for sales beyond successive thresholds.

5. Do you want to spur temporary boosts in sales results?

Temporary increases in compensation can create long-term benefits without long-term costs if they result in new customers who will buy repeatedly. Two common methods are the sales contest and the SPIFF. A SPIFF is a temporary increase in the commission rate paid for whatever kind of sale is being "incented" (e.g., 10 to 20 percent). The concentrated rewards produce concentrated attention and effort by the sales force.

The Bottom Line

To sum it up:

- Select your compensation plan according to what the market pays salespeople and what you want them to do.

- Once you have the total compensation target and the percent salary, select your commission basis (revenue with margin controls) plus adders for more difficult types of sales.

- Finally, choose how to reward the top sellers with a bonus and how to motivate special attention to temporary priorities, such as a new product introduction using a sales contest or SPIFF.

- When candidates for sales positions compare offers, they also consider perks: cars, electronic gadgets, travel allowance, and expense accounts. This is a topic for another day.

Note that the plan must be documented. It is a contract between employer and employee. The plan can be changed based on how effective and how costly it turns out to be, but changes tend to demotivate the sales force because they usually raise targets or reduce payments or both. So changes affecting current staff must be carefully thought through and carefully communicated to avoid creating bigger problems than the ones you were trying to solve!

9.5 Sales Compensation and the Segmented Sales Force

Sales executives are always finding ways to motivate their teams. From new bonus programs with splashy kickoffs to exotic trips to "exciting" sales contests, it seems like no opportunity is missed. And when sales fall short of the targets, the first culprit is always the compensation plan—"let's tweak it again." For sales compensation plan basics, see Article 9.4.

Meanwhile the company worries about controlling sales costs, with good reason. "Sales force compensation represents the single largest marketing investment for most B2B companies…three times more than advertising [for US companies]," according to "Motivating Salespeople: What Really Works," by Thomas Steenburgh and Michael Ahearne, *Harvard Business Review*, July/August 2012.[33]

This HBR article reports on research into how salespeople with different success rates react to different compensation features. It turns out that "one size fits all" does *not* apply to motivating sales performance.

Different Plans for Different Types of Salespeople

Companies can easily *segment their sales force* into stars, laggards, and core performers. The largest segment is core performers, so improving their results offers the greatest opportunity for higher sales, yet most compensation plans ignore the core performer's need to succeed despite competing with the stars.

Core performers produce the best results when goals and compensation have three tiers rather than two, probably because a two-tier structure makes the higher tier seem unattainable and hence not worth working for. The other technique that motivates core performers better is the selection of prizes for sales contests. These employees need to feel they have a chance to win something of value rather than the stars winning everything.

Contests should have more prizes than the number of stars, and the prizes for lower performance should have some quality that makes them different from, not just less of, the top awards. This means no cash awards. If trips are used, different types of trips are recommended (e.g., family trip vs. golf trip). This enables the core performer to value the award for its content, rather than feeling he or she got less than the star.

Laggards need both carrot and stick. The carrot is a *quarterly* bonus. Research shows that near-term "pace-setting" bonuses result in significantly better performance from this group than annual bonuses. The stick is a pipeline of new salespeople, whose presence makes clear the consequences of substandard performance.

Stars are motivated by the upside, so don't cap it! The best way to demotivate stars is to place a cap on commission compensation, because research shows their efforts diminish when the cap is reached. No surprise there! There should be no ceiling on commissions. The other finding was that stars are highly motivated by an increase in the commission *rate* for sales made after their quota has been met ("stepped" commission plan).

All these techniques can easily coexist on one compensation plan, and need to if the company wants to get the most out of its sales force. Like a portfolio of investments, the *sales force is a portfolio of talents*. Designing a plan to consider their differences motivates each segment to achieve more.

9.6 Sales Support Techniques for Sales Success

Revenue from successful sales is the lifeblood of your business, so what can you do to make sure it flows smoothly? Our last few articles have addressed distributors, the sales compensation plan, and the "insight sales" technique, but these cannot *guarantee* successful sales. They are only part of the mosaic.

Even when you have attractive products, competitive pricing, good market communications and promotions, and well-designed sales compensation, your mosaic is incomplete without effective sales support. Too often, *sales support* is the last consideration, when it should be one of the first.

Just as a building needs a frame for support and a craftsman needs the proper tools, your sales channels—distributors and salespeople—depend on sales support to reach their potential. They know this better than anyone, and the best will join your business only if you provide the proper tools. This means sales support is a condition for hiring a high-quality sales force or distributor.

Two Types of Sales Support: Helpers and Tools

Helpers are work groups or functions that enable sales success. These include:

- Lead generation: Finding qualified potential customers for the salesperson to contact. The company can buy lists, hire lead qualifiers and appointment setting services, gather leads at trade shows, and use email campaigns, social media, or executive networks, and other methods. The whole company should consider it their job to find leads for sales.
  - Note: the best leads are those who have bought from you before, so your customer database must be able to identify former and inactive customers. See Articles 10.5 and 10.6.

– Training on both products and sales techniques by skilled practitioners

– Readily available technical support, from product specialists to experts on applications for particular industries

– Customer service that the salesperson can count on to be accessible, helpful, and effective

– Active market communications opens doors for the salesperson. Techniques include advertising, promotions, and public relations. If the prospect is aware of the company, the sales contact has a much greater chance for success.

Tools are documents and software that make the salesperson efficient, knowledgeable, and confident. Some examples include:

– Videos and presentations

– Statements of benefits

– Answers to common objections

– Software calculators to show cost/benefit using the customer's own information

– Computer-aided design (CAD) on the salesperson's laptop, to define the customized application, develop a quote, and communicate requirements clearly to the production department

– Paper and/or electronic leave-behinds: brochures or collateral materials for customer reference after meeting with the salesperson

– Standard proposals and contracts

- Contact management software, often with an email generation feature, to help the salesperson with timely follow-up and keep management informed of progress through the sales funnel. See Article 4.1.

- A portal where the salesperson can see order status, check on his or her own progress toward sales and commission goals, download materials (tools), and request technical or customer service support.

Sales Support Is a Great Investment!

With the right helpers and tools, salespeople close more sales, waste less time on administration, and stay with the company because they feel valued and supported. The top salespeople look for this type of support before joining a company. Thus *sales support is the foundation for an effective sales force.*

Chapter 10: Effective Marketing Communications

10.1 Marketing Communications Plan: Audience, Goals, Tools, Budget

"How do I get more customers?" is always one of the top questions for every small business. You have a great product, attractive pricing, and a folksy way of working that customers are sure to find appealing. But how will they learn all this? To paraphrase the old song, "To know me is to love me"—but how will they get to know you? Effective marketing communications ("marcom") makes everything else in your business work. When "marcom" is missing, your business is facing failure.

Who Is the Audience?

Effective communications starts with understanding your audience. Who are they? What need are they trying to satisfy? Where do they look for solutions? What media do they pay attention to? What presentation style gets their attention? Your audience is your *target market*. You defined them earlier in your business plan—see Articles 2.3 and 2.7.

Goals and Tools

Your first communications goal will be to *inform* the target audience that you are in the business and draw them to your website. Your tools here will be advertising, public relations/publicity, and events. These are considered "mass media," because they are designed for mass consumption and are much cheaper per "impression" than using more targeted, individualized approaches.

The website is your main tool for the second goal: to *persuade* them to choose you rather than a competitor or substitute solution. The website provides for more extended interaction than advertising. It enables you to present the benefits and the options using video, graphics, and even chat, as well as print. It also enables a direct link to purchasing.

Some forms of public relations/publicity, such as articles and speeches at events, also allow the more lengthy presentation that persuasion requires, but they are delivered to a less-differentiated audience than those who actually go to your website. Thus they are really mass media, more useful to spur the search for your website rather than directly persuade anyone to purchase.

You will also use the website to capture buyer contact information, which you will use later to achieve your third goal: to *remind* them to buy again. Reminder communications reach only the buyers as individuals, so mass communications are inappropriate. Direct or individualized media include email, various social media directed to or available to these fans, messages included with invoices, and the more expensive traditional approaches: direct mail, telemarketing, and personal selling. A regular program of communicating scheduled messages to customers is called CRM: customer relationship management.

As you can see, the process moves from a wider market in the informing stage to a very personal and targeted relationship in the reminding stage. Since all these stages are operating at the same time, you will be using different media for these different purposes in an integrated approach. Your messages will be slightly different as well.

This table links communications goals to the marcom mix tools and provides examples for each tool.

Goal	Marcom Tools	Example
Inform	Advertising	• Online: banner; pop-ups; YouTube; email; traditional*
	Public relations/publicity	• Press release, article
	Event	• Speech; sponsorship; sweepstakes
Persuade	Website	• Product/service pages for each target market segment; catalog; videos; success stories; order/pay
	Sales promotion	• Time-sensitive special offer, communicated by any of the other media, plus coupon mailers and coupon websites
Remind	Regular email	• Planned messages matching customer purchase history
	Social media	• Blog; Facebook business page; tweets
	Direct mail/telemarketing	• Renewal offer

*Traditional advertising involves at least seven media choices. The next article will address the best situations for each media type: TV, radio, newspapers, magazines, directories (e.g., yellow pages), outdoor (e.g., billboards), and direct mail.

How Much to Spend?

Obviously, the opportunities to spend money on marketing can quickly exceed the company's marketing budget. How do you decide how much to spend?

A new or growing business should choose its marketing budget by what it takes to get the job done (the "task" method), because failure to do the communications job means the business fails. Established firms can choose a percentage of revenue as their marketing budget, but new entrants cannot, because they do not yet have the revenue base. New entrants have little revenue to start with, so two methods that do *not* make sense for them are "percentage of revenue" and "match the competitors' spending."

New and growing firms must design the campaign first, frugally, and then price it out. If the cost seems unaffordable, they can then consider the cost and communications impact of removing or modifying the less critical elements. The remainder becomes the budget. Will it all be spent? That depends on the results of tests of the various initiatives. All marketers test before full-scale implementation.

Remember your goals. You need to spend enough to get noticed by a large enough share of your target market, despite your competitors' messages. Your name needs to be available or recalled when they are ready to buy, and you will never know when that is. So your marketing must provide some "presence" all the time, occasionally boosted by additional spending to communicate new offers or new promotions or to make a special effort in key buying seasons.

Advertising only sporadically is a common error in small business communications. The brand has no constant presence, so it must reintroduce itself for every episode or campaign. The expense of previous campaigns is wasted rather than establishing a constant base of messaging. During the gaps, the brand is not heard or considered by customers choosing to buy at that time.

Planning market communications starts with understanding the target market, the audience. Next, you select the marcom tool(s) to fit each of your three goals, assess potential cost, modify the marcom tools mix, and select a budget.

Some say market communications can be summarized in six Ms. In this article we addressed mission, mix, and money. The next article considers media. The other two Ms are messages and measurement.

10.2 Marketing Communications Plan: Media

I have a budget, and I cannot do it all. What media do I spend my money on? Consider the strengths and weaknesses of each type of media, and match them to your product and your communications task or goal.

This article addresses your use of traditional media, usually with the goal of attracting people to learn more at your website. It assumes you have a good website, and you are updating it with special offers, pictures of events, videos showing customers enjoying product benefits, success stories, and endorsements. The first thing you should spend your money on is a great website. Then you can spend money on attracting people to view it. See Article 10.3.

Media Strengths and Weaknesses

In this table on media strengths and weaknesses, L (low) is a weakness, M is for medium, and H (high) is a strength.

Media Strengths and Weaknesses	Local	Targeted*	Audio-Visual/ Graphics	Cheap/ Fast	Complex Message**
Network TV	L	L	H/H	L	L
Cable TV	M	M	H/H	M	L
Radio	M	M	M/L	H	L
Metro Newspaper	M	L	L/L	H	M
Local Newspaper	H	L	L/L	H	M
Magazines	L	H	L/H	L	H
Yellow Pages	H	L	L/L	L	M
Coupons	H	L	L/H	H	M
Outdoor	H	L	L/L	M	L
Direct Mail	H	H	L/H	M	H

*By income and/or interest or hobby

**Complex messages require space to tell your story and media that can be saved for later reference.

Network television offers visual presentation, but it costs too much for small businesses, both for the media time and for the production cost of the ad. Cable TV is cheaper, more local, and offers the option of a streaming print for those who wish to avoid ad production costs. However, if you want to choose print, cheaper media are available. Some targeting by type of channel is also possible on cable TV. Neither has the space or permanence for complex messages.

Radio is local and can be targeted by type of station but not by income or interest. It's cheap and fast, but it lacks the space and permanence needed for complex messages. Alternative mobile entertainment seems to be making radio less useful to reach customers.

Newspaper ads can be targeted geographically if local newspapers are used. They offer the space for complex messages but not the permanence for reference unless your customer clips the ad. They are cheap and fast, but look elsewhere if you need quality graphics.

Magazines can be highly targeted by interest and income. They offer high-quality graphics and space and permanence for complex messages. Magazine ads take longer to produce and cost more than newspapers and radio, and their publication schedule cannot handle fast-changing offers.

Yellow Pages is the pre-Internet search option. They are quite expensive and involve lead times of a year or more due to annual publication. Their graphics are poor compared to Internet search.

Coupons can be printed in other media or mailed as part of packages to selected geographic areas. They are now available on Internet coupon sites as well. Cost is low for production but can be high when the cost of the discount is considered. This media makes sense if your objective is to attract interest and "tryouts," in the hopes of more profitable sales later.

Outdoor includes billboards and various types of signage. It is suitable for reminders for impulse purchases of well-known products for a mass market customer base. It does not fit complex messages or targeted markets. Cost and lead time for production and placement are moderate depending on the location.

Direct mail is very targeted and offers excellent graphics as well as permanence. Its success depends on accuracy of the data in the list used. The most targeted lists can be rented from magazines and associations for one-time use. Direct mail is costly, perhaps $2 per piece, and a 2 percent response rate is good, so the cost of a response is really $100. Once you have the list, lead time to implement is moderate. Due to the cost of direct mail, different campaigns are tested for success using different response numbers for tracking. This means that rolling out a full campaign takes several weeks.

Matching Media to Product and Communications Goal

If you have a mass market, you need mass media. However, most small businesses have more targeted markets, at least in terms of locality, especially if you spent a little time defining your target market as previously recommended!

For a goal of inform/persuade, this means that many small businesses will find the best fit with local newspapers, magazines for special interests, coupons, good signage if they have a retail location, and direct mail for high-margin products if tests prove it can be effective.

For a goal of reminding customers to buy again, if you have the customer's contact information, then Internet contact is best. Inexpensive direct mail (postcards) is also a possibility. If you lack that contact information, then local print ads, coupons, and good retail signage are the best places to spend money on traditional media.

10.3 Tips for Your Website

Your website is your most important *communications tool*, so give it your best effort! It's your front door, that critical first impression. Like your mother told you, "You never get a second chance to make a first impression!"

There must be as many articles about creating a good website as there are small businesses in America. This article makes no attempt to recap them all; it simply offers some tips from the author's experience.

The most important tip is this: get a professional designer, but content is *your* job.

Professional Designer

Why use a professional designer? Here's what he or she can do for you:

* Advise on organization of your tabs and pages; viewers appreciate clear and consistent organization and navigation between tabs and pages.

* Provide the graphics that knit all your pages together. This gives your site a consistent "look and feel," which pleases the reader and makes you look more businesslike.

* Solve all the technical issues, such as which host and software to use (e.g., WordPress), provide navigation from one page to the others, and advise on the proper use of mini-apps ("widgets") for special features.
    o Examples of widgets are print versions of pages, Facebook and other social media links, your blog, shopping cart, site-popularity metrics, and contact by email.

- Add the copyright statement

- Advise you on how to be found in search engines, like Google, using keywords/metatags and search engine optimization (SEO) techniques

Find out if your designer would be creating your site by starting from scratch or by using established software (also known as a content management system, such as WordPress). Do *not* use someone who starts from scratch, because you will be paying to reinvent the wheel and be dependent on the developer for updates! Everything you will need is already developed and available. Plus, it is integrated so you can add new features with only a couple tweaks instead of paying for new development.

I am quite happy with the services of Aimee Grover: *aimee@ plaidfish.com.*

Content Is *Your* Job

Do *not* leave the content of the site to your designer. Content is *your* job! It's your reputation and your message. It's worth your time. But help *is* available. Your designer can provide a framework for the site as a whole and for each page, plus some guidelines on what makes great content. Once you've drafted it, you could hire a content editor, too.

1. Start with making a list of your *goals for the site*. Usually these will include:

   A. Communicate my differentiation and positioning—how I add value for customers, better than their other choices.

   B. Provide credibility assurance—why you can believe that my services will meet your needs best.

C. Offer value in the website itself—to attract more new and returning visitors.

On this last point, one of my trusted advisors puts it this way: "The goal of a website should be to create 'Raving Fans.' Connect with them. Get them to subscribe. Add value. Build a relationship. One of the most important goals of any website is to create a mailing list—just because there are so many other ways companies are building relationships with social media that never existed ten years ago."

2. Second, keeping those goals in mind, list the *topic of each page* of your site. Examples include Home, About Us, Product/ Service pages, Contact Us. There can be others as well, such as success stories, descriptions of capabilities, etc.

In your list, show which pages are the main ones—indicated by having a tab at the top—and which ones will fall within one of those main pages. Review other sites to get ideas for what to do and what to avoid, especially competitor sites. Your designer can help with this.

3. Third, *for each page, make a little table* that shows how it will deliver on your goals:

* Positioning message

* Credibility, such as a testimonial quote at the bottom of the page. To create a testimonial, write it *yourself* and then send it to the person you want to quote and ask for their approval.

* Value for visitors, such as a link to a PDF file or PowerPoint presentation or article

- Internal links to other pages on your site, because clicks on these create a higher position in the search engine rankings

- Picture or graphic for that page

- Possibly an interactive element, such as a video, or a link to some survey of interests, or a game

4. Fourth, within this table, *write the text* that you want on that page. Your text will include "placeholders" in the right spot to show the designer where you want the internal links and the links to value-added information. Your designer can help with comments on your draft.

5. Then send the designer all your material: site outline, page tables, graphics files, articles, etc.

6. After the designer incorporates your content into a design with navigation, it is *your* job to proof all the writing, test all the links, and suggest any changes in the graphic design, tabs and page groupings, navigation, color, font, etc. After those changes, you will need to *proof and test* again.

Allow about two to three months for the entire process. Assume a budget around $2,000 to $4,000, aside from video production, though actual cost will depend on hours spent by the design firm. You can minimize those hours by doing much of the work yourself (organizing the site, planning each page, providing ancillary content, making a list of keywords for search engines) and then using the designer to improve it rather than initiate it.

7. Finally, you will want to be able to *update your site yourself* with new information, promotions, or at least to change the copyright

year to show that your business is still active. Keeping the content fresh is a big factor with search engines and to keep visitors coming back. Think of your relationship with your visitors as an ongoing dialog. So have the designer write down instructions for adding files and editing content, and maybe even adding pages. Then test your use of them to be sure you understand.

8. Then monitor how well your front door is doing. *Check the metrics* to see how many visitors you are getting and where they are coming from. Test where you appear when various search terms are entered in Google or other search engines. Modify as needed and as your business or the competition changes!

Your website is the foundation of your communications. All your other communications efforts draw prospects and customers to the website. So make it a priority, and get the professional expertise to build a site that makes you proud!

10.4 Tips for Using Social Media to Market Your Business

Does the world need yet another article on using social media for business? Probably not, but *you* might find value in a bit of summarization and a few tips from experience.

Social media is the exchange of user-generated content over the Internet. It is two-way and interactive. Examples include blogs, Facebook, YouTube, Twitter, and many others.

Businesses use social media as the receiver.

- You can *monitor* what is being said about your industry, your competitors, and your products by signing up for services like Google Alerts and NetVibes.

- You can *respond* to customer concerns on Facebook and with blog articles.

- You can even make *direct contact* with social media users who are complaining about competitors, to offer a better solution. For example, see *"Tweet Me, Friend Me, Make Me Buy," by Barabara Giamanco and Kent Gregoire,* Harvard Business Review.[34]

Businesses also use social media as the originator primarily to build and maintain relationships, which may blossom into sales. You create some valuable information and invite people to view it and respond or use it. When they do, you have access to them for future direct or in-group messages. Hopefully, they become a "community" who share some interest, which you help satisfy and maintain by repeatedly offering more value.

What is "valuable information"? It might be techniques, such as *Business Techniques in Troubled Times.* It could be recipes or product evaluations. Entertainment—humor—is always welcome. It's valuable if your target audience thinks it meets a need, so they decide whether to keep coming back for more. Then, when they are ready to buy what you offer, the relationship ensures that your business will be considered. You don't "sell." You *maintain a presence* by repeatedly offering value.

What Social Media Should You Use?

Many strategies are available. Here is one successful step-by-step approach.

1. **Create a blog** linked to your website. Its graphics should be related to those on your website, and every article should end with a mini-bio, including your website and email addresses. Post a thoughtful article at least once per week, using a calendar to schedule your topics in advance. You will want to invite people to subscribe to your blog (email marketing). See below for other ways to distribute your valuable content.

2. **Create a Facebook business page.** Again, there should be some graphic consistency with your website and blog, and links to your website should appear. Add content daily. Post your own blog article once a week, and post other information the other days of the week. Examples are: events you will be attending; issues you are resolving; links to other excellent blog or other media articles; tips for using your product. Facebook is the preferred social media app for many, so you need to be there.

3. **Create a LinkedIn profile** for business contacts. When you publish your blog, share it on LinkedIn. You can also post your daily Facebook business page updates on LinkedIn as status updates, comments, or new discussions.

4. **Build social media relationships** to expand your network. How? Use Facebook to "like" and comment on posts and other blog articles. Offer comments in LinkedIn discussions. Post your comments on those other blogs as well. Endorse the work of colleagues on LinkedIn. Cite and link to other blogs in your own blog articles.

5. **"Repurpose" your content.** Submit your blog to various blog directories for a wider audience. Do a YouTube video where you describe or demonstrate what you talked about in one of

your blog articles. When you post comments on other blogs or Facebook posts or LinkedIn discussions, include a link to your own blog article.

6. If your business is retail, consider using Twitter to inform your community of specials or other items of interest.

7. Make sure your website and your blog and your Facebook business page all have links (via "widgets") to the various social media where you have a presence. Your website designer can do this for you.

Once you get the pieces in place, the time commitment might be as much as three to four hours per week, if you spend two hours writing your blog article and one to two hours reviewing and commenting on other blogs and LinkedIn discussions.

What Content Should You Provide?

This process for developing relationships online only works if you have valuable content to share. How can you be sure of that?

For your blog, make a list of 20 topics that your customers may find useful. If your blog is a once-per-week event, 52 topics would cover the whole year, and you will certainly find more interesting topics as the year goes on and as you keep listening to the buzz about your industry.

Your blog topic list could include how to use your product, issues related to the need your product satisfies, the history of solutions to this need, potential future developments, community issues, social media issues, other useful new products, and upcoming trade shows/exhibits. You want to write only a page or two, maybe 300 to 1,000 words, so you don't need to know or explain everything about the topic! For bigger subjects, plan a series of articles.

You can supplement this list of topics with issues you come across in other blogs, in newspapers and magazines, in LinkedIn discussions, at trade events, and in conversations with customers and friends. Get input about topics from Google Alerts about your industry or from websites that claim to provide blog topics. See *"Find Great Blog Topics with These 50 Can't-Fail Techniques"* at the Copyblogger blog.[35]

Think about the sequence of topics, and then make a calendar to guide your efforts.

For the content on your Facebook business page, a calendar is again part of the solution. You will want to post daily on this page, so plan to post the same kind of item every week on the same day. For example:

- Mondays you could post something about your calendar for the week showing what you are working on or where you will be this week, stated in a way that shows how this activity can yield benefits for customers eventually.

- Tuesdays you could post a comment on an article or blog you saw, and include the link.

- Wednesdays you could ask a question, perhaps using it as a LinkedIn discussion as well.

- Thursday might be the day your weekly blog posts. It also shows up on this page automatically, because you used the right widget on your blog.

- Friday is a good time for a comment on something that happened this week.

- You can always supplement by posting another comment on an article or blog, reposting an old blog article of your own, or posting some temporary promotion offer, either yours or some other business's.

By the way, you can prepost content and schedule when it appears up to six months ahead. See *"How do I Schedule a Post to Appear on My Page Later?" at Facebook Help Center, Facebook.com.*[36]

This article defined "value" as the attraction in social media and "relationships" as the result. Monitor the buzz as a "receiver," and follow a step-by-step social media "origination" strategy. Schedule content for both your blog and your Facebook business page. Build relationships with likes, comments, and discussions. You don't have to do it all on day one—get started, and see where it leads!

10.5 Customer Database: The Key to Unlocking Revenue

Your customer information is one of your most important business assets, along with your brand, your website, and your unique way of operating. Customer information is the basis of your relationships, which are themselves the basis of your sales.

Two axioms apply here. One is about your target market and finding new customers: *"identify your best customers* and find more like them."

The other is about sales: "*repeat sales* (to current customers) require the least effort and the least cost." Why? Because you don't have to inform these people that your company exists or persuade them to believe in the company's credibility and the product's value.

New customers and low-cost sales are the hallmarks of efficient marketing. Both require that you know the customers you have. Your customer database captures your knowledge about customers and makes it readily available when needed.

How to Use Your Customer Database

If you take a moment to think about how you might use information about customers, then you can design your database to gather and sort the customer information you need for those purposes. Some common uses are:

1. **Communicate with them,** strengthening the relationship so they feel valued and buy more.

Your communications will include periodic messages that may vary according to the type of customer (customer relationship management or CRM), perhaps using Constant Contact or AWeber or some other email marketing system. You will also want to be able to send an email blast to all your customers, as well as send targeted messages about promotions designed for those who buy a certain product or volume. "We miss you" messages are designed to reignite dormant customers.

    – To get customer email addresses, offer something of value in return (e.g., a discount or coupon, article, or e-book).

2. Keep them longer.

Those who have bought several products, or several times, are much more likely to continue to do so than those who have not. They become *"sticky" customers*, resistant to appeals by competitors. A customer database can capture frequency of purchases so you can make special efforts to reward those who buy often (e.g., a loyalty program) and make special offers to motivate others to move into that category.

3. Find more like them.

Profile the segment of your best customers by lifetime purchase volume/revenue, or even lifetime margin. One technique is to define a few categories of customer behavior or value, and place a "category" field in the customer record. Then create marketing programs directed to your best target market.

4. **Forecast revenue** from new customers, and focus your marketing accordingly.

Your revenue or sales forecast can deal with current customers separately from new customers. You can segment current customers by purchase volume per year, using categories as mentioned above. Each segment will have a different average purchase volume, and possibly a different life cycle as well (weeks, months, or years that they do business with you). For example, for one credit card issuer, the customer life cycle was eight years.

When forecasting how many new customers your marketing will generate, you can estimate how many will fall into each of these segments. Then you can forecast revenue from each type of *new* customer according to the average purchase volume of *current* customers in that segment. Design your marketing program to achieve these goals, and adjust it if results do not achieve this forecast.

What Information Goes into Your Customer Database?

Once you create a *customer record*, you can keep it up to date manually or have it updated automatically by integrating it with your point-of-sale (POS) or ordering system. Automated updates enable you to store purchase information easily. The table below matches data elements to update methods.

Data Element/Update Method	Manual	Either	Automated
Customer number (unchanging)	X		
Name and contact info (include email, birthday)	X		
Original marketing source (how you heard of us)	X		
Date of first order	X		
First purchase item	X		
Subsequent purchases/revenue			X
Key upgrades (to a higher-level package; loyalty program)		X	
Date of key upgrade		X	
Cumulative revenue per year		X	
Interest categories (check box; design boxes for products)	X		
Employees connected to	X		
Special events where customer participated		X	
Date relationship or contract ended	X		
Date of most recent purchase	X		
Any critical comments from attitude survey?	X		

Some tips from experience:

– Create your own **unchanging customer numbers.** Don't use a phone number as a customer number, because if the number changes it's hard to link past behavior under one phone number to current behavior under another number.

– **Key product upgrades** may be your criteria to segment your customers. Be sure to make your loyalty program one of these "upgrade" boxes to be checked when they enroll.

– **Interest categories,** gathered at sign-up, may influence targeted marketing messages.

– **Employee connections** might link a customer to an instructor for a dance studio or to a special customer service rep.

– **Special events** participants may be "sticky" customers; this may be a segmentation criteria.

– **End-of-contract date** can trigger "stay with us" offers and reveal life cycle.

– **Date of most recent purchase** can trigger "come see us again" reminders or offers.

– **Critical comments** can guide improvement efforts and influence targeted messages.

– Design everything so it can be sorted by a computer. Do not depend on verbatim or note entries. Instead, anticipate types of entries and set up menu boxes to be checked.

How Do We Do This?

The software can be part of your POS or order system, or a Microsoft Access database, or even Excel spreadsheets. If you use spreadsheets, learn how to use Excel's "sort" function so you can create lists (reports) with the right contents for various purposes. You may even preprogram commonly used sorts/reports, as you do with QuickBooks.

Setting up the process for who updates the database, when, and where is critical. An out-of-date database equals revenue lost and a business flying blind. The owner should be familiar with using the database and extracting reports or sorts. Monthly, review key reports, and make sure new customer data is current when you review your monthly financial results.

The most efficient way to gather the data is to make it part of the order process. Don't delay data entry for a separate update, because this assures that mistakes will be made! Entry will be deferred too long, data will be misplaced, and transcription errors will occur.

Treat your customer database as one of your most valuable assets. Design it thoughtfully, according to how you will use the data. *Design some reports* in advance to help you decide what data you need for each report. Then *design the data-gathering process* and train employees so the information is captured as part of the regular operation of the business. Then use the data to unlock revenues with repeat sales and targeted marketing to attract the most valuable new customers.

10.6 Using Customer Database Reports

The previous article on the Customer Database recommended designing some reports before you design the database, to help you single out the types of data you will want to store in the database. This article provides guidance on how to do that.

What Reports Might Be Useful?

What if you had all the information you needed to "wow" your customers with individualized communications addressed to their needs and showing how important their relationship is to your company? Sales would jump. Customers would stay and come back to buy again. Your marketing would be efficient and effective.

Stay in this dream for the moment, and figure out what *is* "all the information you need" about your customers. How would you organize it into reports or lists for specific purposes? The table below offers some ideas.

By the way, you'll see the term "sticky" in the table. *Sticky customers* are loyal to your company, as shown by their purchase of multiple products or services from you. The more different things they buy from you, the harder it is for a competitor to take your place, because that switch becomes more disruptive as the customer becomes more dependent on his relationship with you.

Sticky customers may also be your most profitable customers, because their new purchases require less marketing effort. They already know and value your business. They are repeat customers. So you want to create more of them!

Report	Purpose
Customer List	Basic list: number, contact info, start date, annual revenue
Sticky Customer List	Most secure customers; find more like them; move others into this list with targeted promotions; show upgrades, events, loyalty club, annual revenue
Dormant Customer List	Revenue opportunities; stimulate buys with targeted promotions; survey for attitude changes
Email List	For email blasts to all customers
Customers by Revenue	Most valuable customers; enables segmentation and targeted promotions
New Customers (by year)	Target list to achieve sticky status; anniversary promotion
Birthday List (by month)	Spur sales with targeted promotion
Contracts Expiring Soon (choose date)	Revenue risk; renew them with targeted promotion
Key Upgrade List	Most valuable customers; upgrade = status; reveals sticky customers; enables segmentation
Interest List	May trigger ideas for targeted promotion to boost revenue
Employee Connection List	Communications to strengthen relationship; establish employee connections to create sticky customer relationships
Event Participation List	Promote your next event to them; candidates for sticky status
Critical Commentors List	Make sure they receive feedback; offer special promotion; monitor their attitude

Designing Reports

Simple reports have a clear purpose, only one primary data element used for sorting (also called sort field or sort criteria), and include additional data elements to enable the user to carry out the report's purpose. Simple reports use only one line per customer, and that line fits on one page, either vertical (portrait layout) or horizontal (landscape layout).

Let's say you want a key upgrade list. Your key upgrades are bronze, silver, and gold product packages or status. In thinking about the sorting, you realize that sorting on three different data elements to make a single list is beyond your capabilities—you need a *single data element for sorting.*

So you design the database to have a "customer package" data element, with valid entries being 3 for gold, 2 for silver, 1 for bronze, and 0 for those who bought a standalone service rather than a package. This enables you to print a customer list organized in *descending numeric order* for this data element, showing your gold customers first, then silver, etc.

Next you decide what other data you want to see on the customer line in this report. Loyalty program membership will be one. Another will be annual purchase volume. Dates of most recent purchase or contract purchase/expiration will be useful. And, of course, customer number and perhaps employee connection and/or email address.

Now you can send emails to encourage renewal or upgrades, and your message can be targeted to recognize the customer's current status. Customers appreciate it when you understand the nature of the customer's relationship with the business, so use this method to get the best success rate for your marketing effort.

Give it a try. Design some reports, and then make sure the data is stored in ways that enable the reports you designed. With experience, you may decide to change some of the formats, especially the additional data elements to be printed on each line.

The important thing is to set up the right data elements at the outset in a way that can be sorted, because you don't want to go back and update the entire database to add a new data element for all your customers!

With the right customer information at your fingertips in well-designed reports, your marketing can be both efficient and effective!

10.7 A Roadmap for Effective Marketing

This article sums up nine articles on marketing in Chapters 2 and 10. The key ideas are:

1. Effective marketing is one of the three crucial elements for survival of a small business. Marketing is more than communications. It includes choosing the right target market; selecting your differentiation and positioning; designing your product, pricing, distribution, sales and service tactics to support that positioning; and then communicating effectively to the right audience within a manageable budget.

2. Today marketing communications ("marcom") starts with the Internet. You will use traditional and social media to draw prospects to your website.

3. Your marketing plan supports a reasonable sales forecast, a key input to your financial forecast.

4. Your customer database is one of your most important assets— the tool for targeted communications to unlock your revenue potential.

The Roadmap

Start Here: Marketing Planning →	Marketing Communications →	Sales Forecast →	Customer Database
The Market Itself: • Need met • Market size • Trends • Target market • Competitive analysis • Differentiation	**Planning:** — Audience — Marcom goals — Tools — Budget (Go to **Media**)	— Units over time — Avg. price — Revenue — Variable cost — Cash cycle (go to **Customer Database**)	— Contents — Reports — Design for reports — Using reports to generate revenue
Strategy and Tactics: • Positioning • Goals • Strategy • Tactics — Product — Pricing — Distribution and sales — Customer Service — Communications (go to **Marcom Planning**)	**Media:** — Traditional media — Website — Social media (go to **Sales Forecast**)		

Summary of the Articles

2.2 The Market Itself: Who are the customers for the need you are meeting? Are you on the right side of the trends affecting this target market? Is your solution different enough from their other alternatives? If not, you will not succeed!

2.3 Marketing Strategy and Tactics: How do you want your target market to think of your company? Can you sum it up in a memorable positioning slogan? Select your goals, and choose an overall strategy for making a dent in this market. Then define your four Ps and customer service plans to support that strategy and positioning and achieve the goals.

2.4 Sales Forecast: How many sales will you make over time? What will they be worth in revenue? How much will it cost to make and deliver those units? When will you spend for production vs. when will you get the cash from sales? Your sales forecast depends on the rest of your marketing planning, and it is critical to your other financial forecasts. Use reality testing to be sure it is reasonable.

10.1 Marketing Communications Plan: Audience, Goals, Tools, Budget: How will you get your message across amid all the clutter of communications that your audience faces every day? How will you inform and persuade prospects and remind current customers to buy again? Will you use advertising, promotions, events, direct mail, and/or social media? How do you decide how much you can afford to spend? Be sure to consider costs for website and social media development, as well as costs to develop ads and buy media time.

10.2 Marketing Communications Plan: Media: What traditional media fits your audience and your product? What does it cost? You want to have a steady presence so you are considered when the prospect decides it is time to buy. Since media can only communicate limited information, you will want to attract prospects to your website where you can tell the whole story. How will you do that within budget?

10.3 Tips for Your Website: This is the front door to your business. Make sure you use a professional designer, but the content is *your* job. Take a disciplined approach to organizing your site, keeping the user in mind throughout. As a small business, one of your most important goals with your website is to communicate credibility. Do that with professional appearance, clear and valuable information, endorsements, and success stories. Learn how to update the website with current information and do so frequently. A stale website makes relationships go stale as well, undermining its basic purpose.

10.4 Tips for Using Social Media to Market Your Business: Social media is about gaining relationships by providing value. Maintaining relationships provides the presence you need to be considered when prospects decide it is time to buy, or buy again. Use multiple social media. Plan your posts with a calendar and "repurpose" your content in various media. Make sure you are listening and build relationships with two-way communications: be active with likes, comments, and discussions.

10.5 Customer Database: The Key to Unlock Revenue: This is your tool to identify your best customers in order to find more like them, as well as to motivate repeat sales, the easiest and most profitable type of sales. Design your customer record to hold the information you anticipate needing for these two goals. Then design your operations to generate and enter that information in the normal course of business.

10.6 Using Customer Database Reports: Before designing the master customer record, design the customer database reports you'll want to use. What will you use them for? What information will you need to make it easy to do that? Consider how the reports will be sorted, and then set up the data elements in the customer record so your reports will be able to find and use that data as envisioned.

It's much harder to add or revise data elements later than it is to build them correctly at the outset. If you do this right, your marketing communications can flow smoothly and efficiently so you'll actually be able to do what you planned to do!

Effective marketing is the key to your success, so take the time to make realistic plans and develop the tools you will need to carry them out. Your business depends on it!

Part Four

Day-to-Day Management and Operations

213

Day-to-Day Management and Operations

A GOOD BUSINESS PLAN, adequate financing, and effective marketing are the seeds for success, but they are just the beginning. Operational excellence keeps customers coming back and generates profits.

Part Four's Driving Concepts

- Most small business owners are experts in the production side of their business, but they are not experts in managing the business.

- Financial and operational results reveal what works and what does not, yet small business owners tend to shy away from analyzing their numbers.

- Percentage of revenue is the critical technique for analyzing financial results.

* Cash flow is the most important number for small business. Accountants don't look ahead. Owners must. A thirteen week cash flow statement is the first thing the bank asks for when you seek relief from the loan repayment schedule.

* Process improvement is a set of techniques to improve profit and customer satisfaction. Start with understanding processes as they are, using a flowchart, also called a "process map."

* Once you see a process laid out on a flowchart, creative thinking can produce substantial profit improvements. Review typical improvement techniques to trigger that breakthrough idea!

* Family employees may lack the skills needed for the position and may have expectations for special treatment. Market-based policies are needed to effectively manage them.

* More operations management techniques will be presented in 2013 articles on the blog *Business Techniques in Troubled Times.*

Techniques Presented in Part Four

Topic	Technique	Content	Articles
Using Your Numbers	Useful P&L Format	Group accounts into a few categories	11.1
	P&L Analysis	Prioritize by percentage of revenue	11.1, 11.2
	Profit Improvement	Drop low-margin products; reduce costs; raise prices	11.2
Thirteen Week Cash Flow Statement	Design Thirteen Week Cash Flow Statement	This is the owner's job; statement design	12.1
	Forecasting Cash	Forecasting knowns and unknowns	12.2, 12.3
	Assessing Cash Flow	Split labor cost; reasonableness check; shop rate	12.4
Process Improvement	Process Map	Understand the process before changing it; some mechanics	13.1
	Big Picture Process Improvement	Limit options; self-perform; resequence; hand-offs; subassembly; computer support	13.2
	Step Analysis Process Improvement	Better equipment; more efficient methods; fail-safe methods; people management; measurements and standards	13.3
Family Employees	Family Employee Issues	Skills; behavior; expectations	14.1
	Using Policies to Manage	Job descriptions; market-based compensation	14.2
	Management Techniques for Family Employees	Values statement; objectives and accountability; major project approval policy	14.3

Chapter 11: Using Your Numbers

11.1 Owning Your Own Business Means Owning Your Own Books

Most small business owners don't understand bookkeeping, QuickBooks, contribution margin, or cash planning, so they shy away from learning how to use their results to improve the business.

Yet when small businesses fail, it's because they run out of cash. Why does this happen, and why do owners allow cash shortages to develop in the first place? Too often, it's because they don't try to understand their numbers.

They assign someone else to "keep track" of the numbers. Unfortunately, bookkeepers are not planners. Bookkeepers look backward, not forward. Owners are the only ones whose job includes using past performance to improve future results, but they usually do not know how.

The owner is the expert on what the business does, spending up to 80 hours per week to make sure the business has effective operations, and maybe even spending some time on getting new customers. Small business owners typically do not make it a priority to understand their numbers well enough to predict their future. Short-term demands make future planning seem like a low priority. Then they run out of cash!

Fortunately, it is not difficult for small business owners to understand their numbers well enough to plan, even without learning software (e.g., QuickBooks) or bookkeeping. Three techniques are all they need.

- First, require the bookkeeper to export the monthly QuickBooks profit and loss report to an Excel spreadsheet, with one column for each month of the year.

- Second, have the bookkeeper reformat the data in Excel into an income statement with a reasonable number of revenue and expense categories (see below), and for each category heading show the "% of Revenue" in that line.

- Third, study where the money goes and create ideas to change those percentages.

Let's look a little deeper at each of these techniques. First, the Internet has dozens of entries telling the bookkeeper how to export data from QuickBooks to Excel.

Making QuickBooks Reports Manageable

In the second task, you are making the QuickBooks data more useful by reducing the number of entries to a manageable number. For *revenue*, you should have a summary line for each product type. Even in a job shop, you can categorize your jobs into types.

The next main category is *variable expenses*, or Cost of Goods Sold (COGS). Your lines for variable costs will be labor (and associated payroll tax and possibly benefit costs), materials, sub-contractors, shipping, and sales commissions. The labor line will include labor costs devoted to production, with nonproductive labor hours shown elsewhere as overhead costs.

The last major category is *fixed* or *overhead expenses*, those that stay the same regardless of production volume. Here is where you will invent headings and summary lines to group costs by type so the number of lines is manageable. Ten categories should be sufficient. For example:

- Nonproductive labor/tax/benefits
- Salary/tax/benefits
- Facility costs (rent, maintenance, utilities)
- Computer costs (hardware, software, maintenance)
- Vehicle costs
- Office expenses (include phone and bank charges)
- Professional services (accountant, legal, consultants)
- Marketing costs (include travel and entertainment)

- Dues and Licenses (professional licenses, conferences, dues, and subscriptions)

- Miscellaneous—but try to keep this minimal!

This is a lot easier to work with than 30 or 40 accounts, most of which say 0 for the month! If it is easier to work with, there is a better chance you actually *will* work on it!

Analyzing the Results

The third technique is analyzing the results. This is the owner's job, and no one else's. Up to this point you have simply been telling the bookkeeper to present the data in a more useful way.

Analysis starts by looking at percentage of revenue for each line. The key line is "contribution" (to cover overhead and provide profit), also called gross margin. This is revenue minus variable costs, or revenue minus COGS to some accountants.

Hopefully this margin is at least 50 percent of revenue. Why? This margin is what you have left after building the product, and its job is to pay for overhead and leave a profit. If your margin is 50 percent and your overhead is 30 percent of revenue, then your pre-tax profit is 20 percent—a good number.

Numbers are the way we keep score. Without them, you can't know if you are winning the game or losing, until it is too late! Small business owners can avoid a cash shortage *without* expertise in bookkeeping. The secret is to present their results in a way that enables planning, using percentage of revenue and contribution margin. In the next article, we will discuss how you can use this data to improve your business.

11.2 The Easy Way to Use Your Numbers, and Survive

"But I hate numbers; I like people," said the small business owner. Then that no-longer-so-friendly banker called to say the loan payments were late, and the owner had to let some of his now-disappointed staff people go. He also had to get stricter with some of those nice but late-paying customers and the ones who always came back for changes and even returns.

What happened? He ran the business like a social club, where relationships are all that matter. But a business needs cash to run. Without cash, the relationships disappear. When cash flow was weak, the foundation was tottering, but he refused to look down there. "Every time I look down there, I have to study things and make unpleasant decisions, so I don't look any more. I just let my accountant look."

If you don't attend to your numbers, your business will fail. You should be *eager* to see how you're doing! And eager to fix any problems so the business can go on. It's not hard to assess your business financial health, if you focus on "percentage of revenue."

You don't need expertise in bookkeeping if your results are presented in a way that enables planning. You want these numbers to stand out: *percentage of revenue* for every line, and the key lines are total *variable costs,* total *fixed costs,* and *contribution margin.* For a good way to present the information, see Article 11.1. With your data in Excel, you can experiment. Copy it onto a new worksheet or save it under another name, and then change the data to see how changes in your business would affect the bottom line—profit.

Sample Analysis: Profit Up 20 Percent!

Assume you want a minimum profit of 10 percent of revenue, which will be something like 7.5 percent after income tax. If your fixed costs are 30 percent of revenue, then your contribution or operating margin MUST be 40 percent of revenue to cover that 30 percent overhead and leave a 10 percent profit.

If you can cut overhead from 30 percent of revenue to 25 percent, your profit goes up from 10 to 15 percent. Review your overhead or fixed expenses to see what changes make sense.

- You'll see that small changes, such as not buying soda for the office refrigerator, have little or no impact.

- If you cut marketing (probably no more than 5 percent of revenue), what will happen to your flow of new customers? Is such a cut worth the risk?

- Maybe you can reduce nonproductive labor hours by changing work schedules. This is always worth examining. If this number is 5 percent of revenue, including payroll taxes, cutting it to 3 percent raises profit by 2 percent of revenue, which is a 20 percent increase in profit from 10 to 12 percent! "Thanks for the raise," says the owner.

Analysis Techniques

Variable costs and revenue are usually the most fruitful areas to consider. The first technique here is to understand the profitability of each product or product type. On a separate worksheet in Excel, consider each product type. Show the revenue for one unit and the variable costs to produce it. Subtract costs from revenue to see product profit, and then show that as a percentage of revenue.

If this product profit is more than 40 percent, covering a 10 percent profit target and 30 percent overhead, great! If it is less, you must do something. Your choices are: raise the price, reduce the variable cost, stop selling it, or accept a profit lower than your target.

- If you stop selling it and you can replace the revenue by selling more of other products, your profit will increase as a percentage of revenue.

- If you can reduce the variable costs for the product, your profit will increase as well.
  - One technique is to pay less sales commission on less profitable products—change your commission structure to be different per product.
  - Another technique is to change your production process. This is the *best* approach, and there are many techniques. They all start with mapping out the process as it is today, and then imagining what might be changed. See Chapter 13.
  - A third technique is to move some subcontracted work in-house to use nonproductive hours, or move some work to other suppliers if you can off-load the associated payroll hours.

- Raising the price is the *fastest* way to improve profitability. A small price change may not be a problem for your customers, yet it will have a major effect on profit. For example, a 5 percent price increase would raise profits from 10 to 15 percent, a 50 percent gain! Even if you lost a few customers, the gain may be worth it. See Article 8.4 "Pricing Tips: Start High; Big Results from Small Changes."

○ You can use Excel to change the price and revenue per product and reduce the number of units sold to see how many sales you could afford to lose yet still be better off.

A word of caution: Be careful of major investments that you hope will solve the problem. Examples include investing in a major machine purchase or a major new marketing program or moving to a larger, newer location. They deserve their own careful analysis of costs vs. likely benefits. Your entrepreneurial optimism might be your own worst enemy with such major commitments!

Your numbers are begging for your attention! They control the life and death of your business. It's not hard, if the numbers are presented the right way. When variable costs, fixed costs, and margins are presented in terms of percentage of revenue, you don't have to be a bookkeeper or love numbers to see what's out of line.

Chapter 12: Thirteen Week Cash Flow Planning

12.1 Thirteen Week Cash Flow Statement

"Cash is king" in a small business. A cash shortage is one of the hallmarks of a business slipping into trouble—a *distressed business.*

The owner's first priority is to pay the vendors whose services keep cash coming in. Bank loans don't do this, so the owner asks the bank to wait for its payments. In response, the bank wants to know the company's prospects for paying in the future. It asks the owner to forecast revenue and costs and predict cash flow using a 13 Week Cash Flow Statement. See *"13-Week Cash Flow Model Creates Clear Communication Channels."*[37]

What Does a Thirteen Week Cash Flow Statement Look Like?

The "statement" is a spreadsheet containing a column for each of the next thirteen weeks. Starting with cash on hand at the beginning of the period (BOP), on a weekly basis it adds cash expected to be received from outstanding invoices, from work in progress, and from new business in the next thirteen weeks. Then it subtracts the cash used to pay for the variable costs for completing such work, and the expected overhead or fixed expenses to be paid during this period. The net is called "cash flow."

The cash flow at the bottom of each week (end of period or EOP) becomes the cash on hand at the start of the next week (BOP). Thus the net at the bottom of each week is cumulative, showing all the expected cash on hand at the end of that week.

Moving from one column to the next is like turning the page in a checkbook register. The first entry is the cash on hand at the end of the previous week. Each week's column is like the page in that checkbook register, with cash at the top, money coming in, money going out, and the cash on hand at the end of the week.

The Challenge for a Small Business Owner

Small business owners usually understand their expenses very well, and they know what is owed them for completed work and work in progress.

Their problem is forecasting new work and new revenue. Their bookkeeper is not a forecaster, and their accountant looks backward, not forward, so the cash forecast becomes the owner's task. Unfortunately, the owner of a small business spends most of his or her time working *in* the business, not *on* the business. They normally rely on others to track the numbers.

When owners have to do the forecast, they feel overwhelmed by the variety of possible work that might come in and the uncertainty of what kind of work will come in during any given week. They know the bank is being reasonable to ask about their prospects, but feel frustration and resentment when asked to predict the unknown!

How does a small business owner predict revenue, costs, and cash flow on a weekly basis? Is there a secret formula? Probably not, but there *are* some techniques that can help you make a reasonable forecast for the coming weeks, whether or not your business is distressed and facing a cash shortage. We'll describe them in the next three articles.

12.2 Thirteen Week Cash Flow, Part 2: Forecasting the Knowns

Uncertainty and the variety of potential developments is the challenge in preparing a thirteen week cash flow statement. But this task has some easy parts, too. The first step is to forecast *known* revenue and costs—outstanding invoices, work in progress, and new work from proposals already submitted. This part of the process has three steps.

1. **Invoices:** Identify the invoiced amounts you have not received yet. Note how much you expect to receive in each week.

2. **Work in Progress:** How much will you invoice for this work in progress? When will you send the invoice, and how much

later will the cash payment be received? Your revenue is booked when the invoice is sent, and this shows up on the "income statement" or "P&L report." But for a cash flow statement, the important date (or week) is when the cash comes in. You cannot pay a vendor with booked revenue! You need cash.

This timing difference between invoice and receipt of cash is the most important difference between the income statement and the cash flow statement.

If you expect to pay out additional cash to complete this work in progress, be sure to add that additional expense to your *predicted cash outflow* for the coming weeks. Use separate lines (rows) in your spreadsheet to show the costs for work in progress separate from the costs of new work you have not started yet.

The typical rows would be materials, labor, and subcontractor expenses; any unusual shipping or packaging expenses; and any sales commissions. These are called "variable costs" or "costs of goods sold (COGS)."

3. **Known Future Work:** You may have already made a bid or proposal, or you intend to. This should be a third set of rows in your spreadsheet. For each of these jobs, use a separate worksheet to estimate the revenue, costs, timing, and percentage likelihood of getting the job. Then you can use a summary on your master spreadsheet.

For this future work, you will need to make some realistic estimates. When will the customer decide? Should you assume he will take the price you bid, or will you need to come down a bit? When will you order supplies and when will you have to pay cash for them? When will you complete the job and invoice it, and when will you receive cash from the customer. If there are "progress payments" along the way, how much and when?

What are your chances for getting each of these jobs? You will multiply each of the revenue and cost figures by this "probability percentage" estimate, making your forecast a more realistic view of the prospects for the business.

Next you will estimate business as yet unknown. We'll cover that in the next article. At this point, you know the format of the thirteen week cash flow statement, and you forecasted the revenue and costs for outstanding invoices, work in progress, and likely new work you already know about.

12.3 Thirteen Week Cash Flow, Part 3: Forecasting Unknowns

To make a realistic cash flow forecast, you must estimate how much *unknown* revenue and cost will happen in the next thirteen weeks, most of which is new business. Nobody can know the future for sure, but nobody has a better foundation for making this estimate than you.

Consider trends, seasonal patterns, probability percentages for new work, and timing for each cash event. Add this to your forecast of *knowns*, explained in Article 12.2.

Base the Future on the Past

The most obvious technique is to assume trends for the last few weeks will continue for the rest of the thirteen week period. You may believe the trends will change, for reasons such as a new sales approach, or a new marketing campaign, or lower prices from a new process that reduces cost. But the bank will doubt your belief and will assume that past trends continue.

Since you want the bank to believe your forecast, resist the urge to assume improvement. Other than a specific change in price or costs you can control, the only other reason to assume a change in the trends of the last few weeks is a seasonal pattern demonstrated in your results from the same weeks for the last two years. If you do not have that data, do not put it in your base forecast.

Option: Handling Uncertainty with Three "Cases"

You have the option of making more than one forecast. You can do a most likely case, best case, and worst case. The most likely case is based on current trends continuing. The best case is where you can show the results of more optimistic assumptions from better marketing or seasonal trends you expect. The worst case would assume a lower "probability percentage" in capturing new business, or higher costs.

The bank is in the risk management business, so you should not expect it to base a loan decision on your best case. In fact, it may decide that your worst case is actually the most likely one!

Making the Forecast

Now that you have decided what trend basis to use, how do you actually forecast? The problem is the variety of products or jobs that you offer. So make your forecast *by product type*.

Define the types of products you may sell in the next few weeks. Using a separate worksheet, estimate the revenue and the variable costs (material, labor, subcontractors, shipping/packaging, and commissions) for one sale of each type and the timing of each cash event—when you pay and when you are paid. Then create formulas for each product type to show the cash effect each week.

For example, if the sale is in week six and the work completes in week eight, the variable costs may be paid for in week eleven and the cash for the work may be received in week thirteen.

Finally, estimate how many (unit) sales you expect for each type, in each week.

On the master spreadsheet, enter the estimated unit sales per product type per week and enter your formulas for cash in and out for each week for that product type. Sample formula: 50% of Type A sales from week (x) plus 30% of Type B sales from week (y).

In the next article, we will address job shop complexity and how to double-check your work and draw conclusions. Up to this point you have learned how a thirteen week cash flow statement is built, how to forecast the knowns, and how to estimate future revenue and costs for jobs as yet unknown.

12.4 Thirteen Week Cash Flow, Part 4: Forecasting Complexity and Conclusions

When developing a thirteen week cash flow statement in a *job shop*, forecasting future business seems especially difficult due to the variety of jobs that might be won in future weeks. The solution is to select a few typical *product* or *job types* from experience and forecast those as representative of the type of work that might come in. Choose job types significantly different from each other.

For example, 60 percent of the work might be small parts you have built before, 30 percent might be new jobs with simple designs, and 10 percent might be new complex designs. Probably the more complex jobs will have longer durations so that you incur cash costs but do not receive cash payments during the thirteen week period. You might use different percentages if you choose to do best case and worst case scenarios, too.

Is Your Forecast Reasonable?

Once you have a forecast, check it to see if it is reasonable. How does it compare to your cash flow from prior weeks? It should not be radically different.

Do you have enough labor to do the work you forecasted? Do you have enough space and machine time? Does the forecast imply more time spent on quotes and selling than you yourself have available, given the time you will be spending on production and perhaps bank negotiations?

Split Your Labor Cost

A common error is *double counting or under counting labor*. Many company bookkeepers show all payroll as a "fixed" cost because that is the easiest way for them to calculate payroll taxes. But that means you cannot know the margin per product, because you don't assign the labor costs to the product.

Part of your payroll is a variable cost, that is, labor requirements per job or task. Since employees always have some paid time not assigned to particular jobs, a reasonable forecast will need to show nonproductive labor time and cost as an overhead or fixed cost, separate from labor hours assigned to jobs as variable cost or COGS. Payroll taxes should be split the same way.

Nonproductive labor time can be as much as 45 percent, so this is important! Your accounting software (e.g., QuickBooks) entries showing payroll as a fixed cost are only a starting point. Use Excel to split payroll into productive and nonproductive components to forecast margin and cash flow by product type.

Drawing Conclusions

The business owner should draw two types of conclusions from the cash flow forecast: product profitability and business viability.

Analyzing the cash flow by product or job type as described in Article 12.3 shows you the margin per product before overhead. If overhead is 30 percent of total company revenue and your product generates a 30 percent margin (revenue less variable cost /revenue), then you break even and have no profit.

In this example, if you want a 15 percent profit before tax, your products must generate a 45 percent margin on average. If they don't, you must reconsider your price, perhaps raising your "*shop rate,*" or discontinue products that fall short of the target profit. See Article 8.5 for guidance on calculating your shop rate.

Business profitability depends on product profitability, as above. The bank asks for a thirteen week view because it knows that a near-term forecast is more reliable than long term. But the business owner who has long-duration jobs often decides to forecast cash flow for six months (twenty-six weeks) to be able to see the cash payments for long-duration jobs rather than just the costs. In this case, a longer view is needed to get the most realistic picture of business viability.

Forecasting cash flow from unknown future work in a job shop can be done by choosing representative product or job types. Key issues include double counting or under counting labor, nonproductive labor time, shop rate, and margin per product or job type.

Chapter 13: Process Improvement

13.1 Improving Profits by Process Improvement

One of the best ways for small business to improve profits is changing processes to use less variable costs: less labor or materials, less subcontractor cost, less shipping cost. The result is a higher contribution margin.

Process improvement is the *best* technique for profit improvement because it produces more profit with *every* sale. Unlike a reduction in fixed costs, process improvement generates more and more profit as the business grows. Unlike a price increase, it does not threaten sales volume.

Process improvement increases the contribution or operating margin, in both dollars and percentage of revenue. As sales increase, profit increases, while fixed costs stay the same. Profit becomes a higher and higher percentage of revenue, while fixed or overhead costs become a lower and lower percentage of revenue.

The goal is a substantial change in profit, so look for changes with substantial impact!

Start with a Flowchart: The "Process Map"

Process improvement starts with understanding the process itself. The best way to do that is to map the process using a flowchart— a *process map*.

You can draw this process map by hand, or use a Microsoft Office program called Visio, or even PowerPoint. A good tutorial on process mapping can be found at *Balanced Scorecard's Handbook for Basic Process Improvement,* especially pages 21 to 24 in the PDF page count.[38]

This technique works well for both service businesses and production environments. In a job shop, you will start with your bill of materials (BOM) and routing sheet. Of course, you will want to make sure they are accurate first!

Your goal for process improvement is *substantial change*. You want to reduce the costs and time involved by 25 to 50 percent or more. A faster process reduces inventory holding costs as well as labor hours, and may improve cash flow as well. Faster production can also be a competitive advantage.

Process Map Techniques

To improve your process, pay special attention to opportunities to reduce customization, hand-offs, inspections, and approvals. These all introduce delay and overhead. To enable this type of examination, make sure your process map displays each of these time-wasters as they exist in your process today.

The first version of your process map will show the movement of materials and all the major steps of processing them, all the way through shipment. You will show branches for options and decision points as diamonds, with yes/no branches leading to various alternative outcomes.

The second version of your process map will add notes to show how long each process step takes, how long production waits between steps, and what percentage of the jobs use each branch (such as rework after inspection). It is also a good idea to show the flow of paperwork generated by each step.

Process improvement is the route to substantial change in variable costs and long-term profit. It starts with a process map so you can see what might be changed. The next two articles will explain eleven techniques for improving your processes.

13.2 Big Picture Techniques for Process Improvement

Article 13.1 described how to map out a process for a service business or a production environment. Assuming you have done that, you are now ready for *process improvement*—examining today's process for opportunities to simplify, improving profits substantially. This article describes some techniques for doing so.

First, consider the process as a whole. How can you make it simpler?

Limit Options: Customization and variety introduce complexity. They create multiple branches in the flow. Consider how often customers choose a particular variation. If the answer is seldom, consider withdrawing that option. What do competitors offer? Is your variety crucial to your competitive advantage, or is it simply a legacy not considered valuable by most customers?

Self-Perform: Are there steps in your process that could be done by the customer himself when they order, or after receiving your product? This is one way to simplify your process, especially in a service business. Examples are IKEA, and call center voice menus where callers direct themselves to the correct group of agents.

Resequence: Are materials being moved significant distances in your facility between steps? This time and effort is waste, because it does not add value for the customer. How could you make this simpler?

Hand-offs: When work moves from one workgroup to another, the new workgroup does not attend to it immediately. The work joins a queue, and the time waiting in queue is a waste. What if you created a "work cell" able to perform more than one set of tasks so that a hand-off is avoided?

Subassembly: Is there one part of one step in the process that could be done independently of the rest, on the side, so that its work product could be introduced in semicomplete form when and where it is needed? This subassembly technique works especially well when these tasks use special skills or equipment, which need not be located in the "main line" where the finished product is assembled. Many companies use work cells to build subassemblies.

Computer Support: Consider your paperwork flow. Rather than sending paperwork to a clerical group that enters data, you could have data entered by the people doing the work at the time they do it. This saves time, avoids transcription errors, and eliminates the need for the clerical group to seek clarification of illegible or missing entries. Immediate data entry also displays current progress to those working on subsequent steps.

Is your computer system set up to give you the historical data you need to see trends in the business so you can plan? If not, find a way to capture what you need for the future when it is happening in production.

Use these techniques to redesign the process as a whole, with the goal being substantial change in profit. The next article explains more techniques to improve profits by improving the longest steps within your processes.

13.3 "Step Analysis" Techniques for Process Improvement

After considering process improvement opportunities by simplifying the process as a whole (see Article 13.2), *examine each of the longest steps in the process map* to see how they can be improved. Remember, you are seeking substantial change in costs and speed. The result will be a higher profit margin. Consider equipment, methods, measurement, and people management.

Analyze the Longest Process Steps

Better Equipment: Is one machine a *bottleneck*, with work queued up in front of it and idle resources waiting for work beyond it? If so, you must find a way to optimize this step. If you have the capital, there may be faster machines or you may buy a second machine. If you lack the capital or do not wish to take on more risk, there are still techniques available.

Are there any jobs that use this machine but need not do so? Can some work using this machine be outsourced? Inspect any parts before they use this machine so you are not wasting machine time on defective units.

Is the machine maintained outside of production hours? It should always be operating despite breaks and lunches. Use small lot sizes to retain flexibility for high-priority jobs. Find a way to reduce setup time for this machine to a minimum, because it cannot be processing during setup.

More Efficient Processing Methods: Remove unnecessary steps. Defer or remove steps that add value for only a small percentage of the units. Avoid multiple inspections—workers at each step should inspect their own work to minimize rework. In addition, work cells and subassemblies can be used to re-assign work so it can be done more efficiently.

Fail-Safe Methods: Design tools and supply kits so mistakes cannot be made, similar to "edit-checks" for valid data entry to software. Examples are tabs on jigs, parts that can only be fitted the correct way, or supply kits with a gaping, empty spot for each necessary part. The Japanese call this "*poka-yoke,*" with a meaning something like "idiot-proof."

People Management: Get out of your office and observe your people regularly to make sure they actually know how to do each task correctly, and coach them on the right methods. Provide job aids showing the proper sequence with photos of right way/wrong way.

Provide incentives for quantity balanced with quality performance. Make sure overtime to do rework does not become an incentive to perform poorly on the first pass. Provide a clear visual signal to identify priority jobs, to be used by workers who need help to finish on time.

Measurements with Standards: For each work operation, establish quantity, quality, and time standards. If you don't make your expectations known, how can the staff meet them? Monitor the results. When you see a negative trend, personally observe and coach the worker on how to meet standards. Reward those who consistently exceed quantity standards with good quality.

Efficient processes generate profits. The first set of techniques addresses the layout or design of the process as a whole. Then you examine individual process steps, where the levers for change all start with M: materials, machinery, methods, measurement, and management of the people doing the work.

Chapter 14: Family Employees

14.1 Employing Family

Small business owners often resort to employing family members because they are available, known, and trusted. But workplace problems are more difficult to solve when they involve family members, requiring special attention to management tools and techniques.

Relationship Issues

The word "family" is positive. It conjures up images of teamwork that are wholesome, loyal, friendly, etc. Many employers talk about their workforce as family. But anyone who is actually in a family–that would be most of us!—has felt family discomfort, too. All the relationship issues in real families crop up in workplace families: sibling rivalry, feeling unappreciated, expecting forgiveness for repeated trespasses.

When the workplace family has some real family relationships as well, there are some rewards, but the risks resulting from dysfunction can be many times more serious. This risk is multiplied again where there are only a few employees—when the teapot is smaller, the tempest brews more quickly and explosively. And who does the most family hiring? You guessed it—the companies with the fewest employees: small business.

The Best Person for the Job

Why hire family? As Willie Nelson sang, "I've got a long list of real good reasons…" Some are trust; the devil you know; loyalty (he needed a job); tax benefits; and the expectation that family will be committed and willing to sacrifice from time to time when the business needs it.

Unfortunately, one does not often hear that the family member was the most competent candidate: "I needed a marketer, and my son Bill is the best marketing guy I've ever met." Small businesses live on the edge. They are the businesses who can least afford mediocre employees. Small businesses need committed multitalented people.

What Can Go Wrong?

The reasons to avoid hiring family are mostly about what can go wrong. The employee might feel exploited and let that dissatisfaction show, poisoning the workplace atmosphere. Managing a family employee is only easy when it is not needed! Correcting and coaching a family member is a touchy area that can spark issues outside the office on the home front.

Family employees may have issues from home (arguments, rivalries, jealousies) that they cannot ignore when they work with the same people. Nonfamily employees feel out of the loop and less influential when they must compete with family members for the boss's ear. They may also perceive unfair treatment compared to a family member, in terms of privileges or pay compared to competence and/or effort.

What should a small business do? Should it take advantage of the obvious benefits of depending on a trusted family member, especially when there are some tax benefits involved? Or should it avoid family employees to avoid the extra-difficult morale and relationship issues that result when all is not rosy? Are there some tools that a smart small business can use to employ family yet minimize the downside risk?

Yes, some techniques are available. The next two articles explain them.

14.2 Using Policies to Manage Family Employees

One of the toughest challenges for a small business is finding competent and reliable employees. When you find one and they are family, why look further? See Article 14.1 for some pitfalls. Managing family employees can be difficult. Techniques to make it easier include job descriptions, market-based compensation, and other market-based policies.

Establish Company Policies

According to some owners, there are many reasons to establish a policy of never hiring family members. Article 14.1 cited some. Other reasons range from "simultaneous vacations are too disruptive" to "family members who believe they are immune to termination may even work together to frustrate the boss's goals."

Unfortunately, these potential problems are unconvincing to the child or sibling or to a good employee recommending his relative. They see the immediate need, not the future risks.

"*Market-based policies*" may be the best tool for a small business faced with family employment issues. Larger businesses have traditionally "established a policy" to handle potentially contentious issues in a consistent way. In contrast, small businesses often perceive policies as big company overhead and bureaucracy, the very thing they try to avoid in their own business.

The benefits of establishing a policy are: 1) you can spend your time more productively because you don't have to invent an answer every time the same problem arises, and 2) you don't have to deal with accusations of favoritism and inconsistency each time you make a new decision on the same subject.

Job Descriptions

One example of a market-based policy is that every job will have a "job description," citing responsibilities, duties, and qualifications. These provide a reason to reject mediocre relatives and a way to control disputes about responsibilities when the fairness and blame games begin.

Market-Based Compensation

A job description is also the foundation for a market-based compensation structure, which can control the inevitable favoritism complaints when family members are employed. Once the responsibilities and qualifications are in writing, you have the opportunity to find the market price for such an employee. This becomes the benchmark for compensation—the market—not whether you like me! *Salary.com* is one source for market-based labor rates by job title. You can localize it per ZIP code.

Rates of pay can vary from the marketplace norm for clear reasons, such as including a family member's equity interest as part of their compensation, or additional responsibilities delegated to a family member. As long as the compensation is based on clear responsibilities and qualifications and their worth to other employers, you have a chance of resolving matters on a logical rather than emotional basis.

14.3 Management Techniques for Family Employees

Family employees can be a problem as well as a blessing. Establishing policies makes sense even for a small business. Address the problem once, write down the answer as a policy, and move on. Aside from job descriptions and a market-based compensation plan, other useful techniques include objectives, accountability, shared values, and even a major project approval process.

Agree on Objectives

Imagine you employ your spouse, and he or she does the finances. You want him or her to produce the end-of-month reports by the fifth business day, not the fifteenth. When you ask for that, the response is a litany of how he or she spends their time.

What is missing here is a list of goals to be accomplished, agreed to by both parties at the beginning of the year. Your finance person needs to deliver the reports when you need them.

They have to figure out how to do that rather than telling you their problems and, by implication, asking *you* to manage their time. This is *their* problem to solve, not yours. You care about the deliverable, not how they manage their time.

The tool is agreed goals. Without them, there is no basis for the subordinate's accountability.

Write Down the Company Values

The same idea can take the form of *behavior expectations, commonly called "values."* These are "the way we do things around here." Examples: we value teamwork; our integrity is never compromised; we deliver what we promise, to each other as well as to customers and suppliers; our behavior makes our colleagues proud.

It may seem silly to write down behavioral expectations, but it is most important when you employ family. Why? Because family members have a history of behavior outside the workplace, and they may expect to behave the same way at work—after all, you know them.

They may also believe there are no consequences for inappropriate workplace behavior if one is family, setting up a double standard when nonfamily employees are considered. The best way to handle this is a set of standards communicated (hence, in writing) before any problems arise. Like goals, these provide a basis for accountability and consequences.

Major Project Approval Policy

One other "policy" could serve small business well: a "major project approval policy." A major project is usually a large investment, such as a marketing program or a new machine or moving the business. By thinking in advance about what would justify taking such a risk, you improve communications with any co-owner or family member who may be affected by the decision.

Prior definition of decision criteria can also help you as the decision-maker, bringing a degree of dispassionate logic to what may be an emotional issue, with hope warring against fear, or courage facing down prudence.

Problems with Policies

For a small business owner, the unfamiliar behavior here is thinking about potential business problems *before* they arise and writing down a framework of expectations, or solution criteria. These owners normally don't feel they have enough time to handle immediate problems, let alone anticipating issues that might come up in the future!

Also, they are not comfortable committing to written policies, because they know the future brings change and they will need flexibility. They might see policies as an obstacle to managing their future rather than a tool for organizing their chaotic lives.

Managing employees is not easy, and family employees redouble the stress involved. Establishing and enforcing policies is the key to success: qualifications, job descriptions, shared values, objectives, accountability, market-based compensation, and a major project approval process.

Growing and Exiting Your Business

Growing and Exiting Your Business

G ROWTH AND EXIT are two business issues that go beyond day-to-day operational demands. These two issues can add tremendous value for the business and its owners, but small business owners tend to focus on the near-term issues, leaving these more "transformational" challenges to be dealt with later.

Part Five's Driving Concepts

* Identifying the most profitable segments of a business can be used to reshape it: attracting more of the best customers; selling more of the most profitable products; spending less time and money on low-margin segments.

* More growth techniques will be presented in 2013 articles on the blog *Business Techniques in Troubled Times.*

* The value of many small businesses is dependent on the role of the owner. This means that owners should not expect to reap large rewards by selling their business when they

want to retire. Instead, they should manage the business to build up retirement funds while it is operating.

* Progressively selling the business to employees via an ESOP (Employee Stock Ownership Plan) is one increasingly popular method for building retirement value during the operating years.

* More exit techniques will be presented in 2013 articles on the blog *Business Techniques in Troubled Times.*

Techniques Presented in Part Five

Topic	Techniques	Content	Articles
Growth through Focus: Pruning	Segment by Margin	Segmentation; focus on winners	15.1
	Pruning Process	Nine steps; what can go wrong; old way/new way	15.2
Employee Stock Ownership Plans	Simple ESOP	Definition; distributions; control; costs; tax benefits; advantages/disadvantages	16.1
	Leveraged ESOP	Definition; use of funds; loan; structure and benefits; getting started	16.2
	ESOP Lessons Learned	Company administration; setup time/cost; professional administration; control; distribution issue	16.3

Chapter 15: Growth through Focus: Pruning Your Business

15.1 "Growth through Focus": Pruning Your Business

Every business seeks growth, especially small business, where a few new customers can cover the overhead and transform loss into profit. The owner tries a new marketing message, or goes after a new market, even if it means new products. He or she is not afraid to customize to get one new customer or may even come up with a new brand for a second identity.

Finding the Profitable Parts

Experts in turning around businesses take a different approach. Before expanding, they seek understanding.

Turnaround experts ask "what works today, and what does not?" They look at the margins of products or product lines, customer groups, geographies served, and production processes. Usually owners have never analyzed these segments of their business, and the results can be astounding!

Armed with this segmented margin analysis, turnaround experts work with the owner to decide on one more input: what margin do you need to meet your goal of saving or expanding the business? Knowing that, they can see which segments meet the target. You want to do more of those! Find more customers like those customers, make more products with that process, sell more into the best geography or find similar areas.

"Segment margin analysis" usually leads to figuring out how to fix the laggards. That's natural but typically results in minor gains, if any. It is often more effective to push the laggards aside for the moment and focus instead on doing more of what works. Celebrate these successes, and find ways to do more of them! Spend your time and money on success, not rehab.

Focus Resources on the Winners

The segments with margins below target call for improvement or cancellation. If you work on improving them, as you probably have already been doing, your attention and resources are devoted to them rather than to growing the successful segments.

On the other hand, if you decide to close them down, the time and money you spent there can be re-invested to grow the successful segments. If there is a quick fix with major results, great! Otherwise, you must decide when doing more of the same and hoping for different results is a triumph of heart over head. You already know what works well! Concentrate resources where your company has the best chance of winning.

The following is from *"Growth through Focus: A Blueprint for Driving Profitable Expansion,"* by Khosla and Sawhney in *Strategy and Business:* "…growth often comes from fewer but stronger arrows aimed at fewer targets. The engines of growth are focus (fewer brands, fewer categories, fewer markets) and simplicity (simple vision, simplified execution, and simpler organizational design)…complexity is an avoidable enemy of growth."[39]

Fewer arrows and fewer targets implies a different vision for your business. See Chapter 1 for techniques to re-develop the vision.

The next article will address some techniques for growing your business through focus.

15.2 Techniques to Prune Your Business

The road to profits is one of focus and simplicity. Owners must understand which products, markets, customers, or processes have been winners for the company, and focus on them while shedding or starving the losers.

It's a strategy of "more through less." When everyone in the company understands what makes a winner, you avoid distractions, gain focus, and improve margins.

Here is a process for focusing on the winners:

1. **Identify the segments:** Get your people together so they become part of the process from the beginning. Ask them to help you make a list of types of products, customers, geographic areas, processes, and distributors where margins might vary.

2. **Gather your data:** Understand the margins for each type of segment they identified. You "understand" when you know *why* the margin is what it is: the cost components, your price, and your position vs. competitors.

For example, maybe you are spending money for quality that really doesn't matter to some or even to all customers. Also, take some time to think about how your fixed expenses (overhead) might change if you did not serve that type of segment.

3. **Get their ideas:** Meet with your people again, and share your findings. Some owners shy away from disclosing numbers to their people, but you cannot get them involved without trusting their discretion and judgment, and you need them involved because they, too, must focus.

When the discussion turns to what can be done, after some time for venting and excuses, steer the discussion away from fixing the laggard segments. Spend your and their time on how to *develop the winners* more and find more like them. The outcome should be an easel list of possible initiatives to do just that.

4. **Assess "success themes":** After a break, or another day, provide the team with a grouping of the ideas into types of growth activities, or "success themes." Examples might be relationship-building with potentially strong customers, or changing a product or process, or marketing efforts to find a particular type of customer.

Then ask the team to help place these success themes on a *nine-cell grid:* one axis is expected impact, and the other is ease of implementation, i.e., effort and resources required. Your high-medium-low break points can be dollars or hours, or even unstated. See Article 1.5.

5. **One level deeper:** Your team was thinking and talking about implementation while they made the assessment. Capture that energy and thinking before you end the meeting.

Use two of the more attractive themes, and brainstorm *three levels of action* for each. The first operates as a trial, the second extends the effort, and the third is a full-scale effort. This makes the assessment real and can result in changing the placement of the theme on the grid as everyone understands it better.

6. **Assign champions:** As the meeting ends, assign themes to individuals and ask them to work with you on developing an implementation plan for each: tasks, timelines, and participants.

7. **Bring it together:** After a week or two, you will have the implementation plans. In the meantime you will have assessed what resources can be freed by *starving the laggard segments*. You'll also have reviewed your sources for additional skills and money.

At this point, you earn your pay. You decide what will be done with what resources, who will do it, and when it will be done. You also decide how the laggards will be starved. Put a catchy name on your new strategy, and call another meeting to explain it all and listen to reactions.

8. **Make it happen:** It's your job to free up the people, hire the skills, provide the money, stop doing business as usual, and celebrate the initial successes. This is where you earn credibility. Your focus will be simple and clear for all to see.

9. **Measure progress:** You owe it to yourself, your team, and your business to keep track of whether the changes in activities are changing the numbers. Figure out which measurements will show that, track them at least weekly, and share them with the team. Adjustments will be needed—don't be afraid to make them quickly.

What Can Go Wrong

* You *must* fix underlying problems before building scale. This should be part of the implementation plans.

* Managing the laggards: you can milk them for margins while reducing their use of resources, or you can divest (sell them or close them down), or you can leave them alone because they make a contribution to profits but cannot be extended as a success theme. Radical action shows you are serious about focus and simplicity, but a case-by-case analysis of these segments will be part of your resource planning when you "bring it together."

* You may not "stay the course." Then you are back where you started.

Pruning your business means envisioning a transformed business built on what works. That new business is your vision. A great technique for showing what's different is to make a chart listing key aspects of the business and then showing *"old way"* followed by *"new way"* for each. For more on defining your vision by key aspects of the business, see Chapter 1.

Acknowledgement: This article was inspired by *"Growth through Focus: A Blueprint for Driving Profitable Expansion,"* by Khosla and Sawhney in *Strategy and Business*, Autumn 2010.[40]

Chapter 16: Employee Stock Ownership Plans (ESOPs)

16.1 Employee Stock Ownership Plans (ESOPs) and Small Business

An ESOP creates a market for the shares of a privately held company, enabling an owner to retain control while selling ownership gradually to employees using tax-deductible company funds. Meanwhile employees gain ownership of the company they work for and build a retirement fund, while putting up no cash.

Employee Stock Ownership Plans (ESOPs) are an increasingly popular way to combine the objectives of employee retirement benefits, employee loyalty, and tax-advantaged buyout of owners (*exit strategy*). They can also be a flexible tax-advantaged source of company financing for internal purposes, an acquisition, or divesting a subsidiary.

The first ESOP was formed in 1957. By 2008, over 11,000 ESOPs were operating with over 13 million members and over $500 billion in assets. An excellent source is NCEO: the National Center for Employee Ownership (see *National Center for Employee Ownership (NCEO): ESOP plans, stock options, restricted stock, phantom stock, and more*).[41]

Basic Definition

An ESOP is a tax-qualified, defined-contribution, employee benefit plan, like a profit-sharing plan or a 401(k) plan. Unlike other such plans, ESOPs are designed to be able to invest primarily in the stock of the employer company and are permitted to borrow money to finance their purchase of the employer's stock. Both C and S corporations are permitted to sponsor ESOPs.

To enable the ESOP to purchase the employer's stock or to repay a loan used to purchase the employer's stock, the employer makes annual tax-deductible cash contributions to a trust: up to 25 percent of payroll if the ESOP does not borrow money to purchase employer stock, plus an additional 25 percent if the ESOP borrowed money to do so.

The trust uses the cash to buy company stock or repay the loan used to purchase employer stock, and then allocates the shares to individual employee accounts within the trust. Allocations are made according to a formula using compensation, years of service, or both.

Distributions to Employees

Like all other ERISA-qualified plans, employees gain the right to own the shares over a vesting period as long as six years, and they can receive a distribution of either the "vested" shares or their cash value after leaving the company.

Timing of distributions depends on the reason the employee left the company and the terms of the plan document. An ex-employee may be able to receive a distribution of his or her ESOP account or its cash value:

(i)   immediately, in the event of a retirement

(ii) one year following death or disability

(iii) up to five years following termination for reasons other than death or retirement

Ex-employees may then sell the shares and pay applicable taxes and any applicable penalties, or "roll over" the shares or their cash value into an IRA without incurring any taxes or penalties.

If the shares are not publicly traded, the ex-employee who receives shares can require the company to buy the shares back for the fair market value of the shares at designated times during a two-year period following the distribution.

The company, if not publicly traded, hires an appraiser to determine the fair market value of the shares each year. This appraisal not only establishes the price at which the shares are first bought but also the price at which an ex-employee may sell the shares back to the company.

For the ex-employee's taxes, unless the ex-employee "rolls over" his or her distribution to an IRA or an ERISA-qualified plan, the value of the shares when they are sold becomes ordinary income, like a distribution from a 401(k) or IRA. A 10 percent penalty applies if they are sold before the ex-employee is 59.5 years old.

ESOP and Control

An ESOP trust is created and owns the shares in the ESOP. A trustee administers the trust and has the power to vote the ESOP's shares. However, the participants may direct the trustee how to vote shares allocated to their accounts on major corporate issues and on other matters where the plan document permits them to vote.

Since the trustee is appointed by the board and anyone can be appointed to serve as trustee, the owner or a company executive often serves as the trustee until a "conflict of interest" arises. This mechanism enables the company's owners to retain control. In the event of a conflict of interest, a more "independent" trustee is often appointed.

ESOP Costs

The cost of setting up an ESOP and completing the ESOP's initial stock purchase ranges from a low of $40,000 for the design and implementation of a simple plan that does not incur debt to finance its purchase of employer stock, to as much as $150,000 or more, depending on the complexity of the stock purchase and the financing transaction.

Costs to be covered include: 1) the trustee and his/its attorney and appraiser, 2) the company's attorney and accountant, and

3) the bank's fees and the cost of its attorneys, if a bank provides the financing for the stock purchase.

Ongoing costs should be in the range of $10,000 to $15,000 annually, covering fees for plan administration and recordkeeping, legal advice, and the annual appraisal.

Tax Benefits for Owners and Company

The shares purchased by the ESOP may be newly issued or may be bought from the owners. If one of the company's owners sells at least 30 percent of their shares in the company to an ESOP and the company is taxed as a C corporation, the selling owner is permitted to defer paying taxes on the gain if the owner invests the proceeds in US stocks (not funds).

The tax that would otherwise have been due and payable at the time of sale is deferred until the US stocks are sold. Then the proceeds are taxed at capital gains rates. If this "replacement property" is not sold prior to the owner's death, the owner's heirs can receive it at a tax-basis value equal to its value at the time of the owner's death.

This means heirs would not pay tax on any gain in the value of the sold shares or any increase in the value of the replacement property that the deceased owner would have had to pay otherwise. This capital gains tax benefit is not available to owners of S corporations.

While S corporations are limited to 100 shareholders, since 1999 ESOPs have been permitted to be an owner of the stock of an S corporation and, regardless of the number of employee participants, the ESOP is counted as only one shareholder.

As will be explored in a later article, if a transaction is properly structured so the ESOP owns *all* of the S corporation's stock, the stock of the company is then owned by an ERISA-qualified trust, which is a nontax-paying entity. As a result, the company can become a "for-profit, nontax-paying entity," exempt from paying federal income taxes as well as state corporate income taxes in most states.

As noted throughout this article, an ESOP can borrow money and use it to buy shares. This approach, called a "leveraged ESOP," will be discussed in more detail in Article 16.2.

Advantages and Disadvantages

The table below shows the effects of the basic ESOP concept on all concerned, excluding more complicated strategies such as a leveraged ESOP.

	Advantages	Disadvantages
Employee	Ownership; retirement funds; no cash outlay unlike 401(k)	Funds not diversified as they could be in 401(k)
Company	1. "Performance based" retirement plan (i.e., the value of the employee's retirement plan will reflect the performance of the company, rather than the value of the stock of unrelated publicly traded companies) 2. Employee loyalty 3. Contribution is tax deductible 4. Smooth succession and business perpetuation planning 5. Selling owners still can retain control	1. Cash will be needed for future share buyback if shares are not publicly traded at time of repurchase 2. Cost for ESOP initially and annually 3. Ongoing costs for compliance with often-changing tax and ERISA regulatory requirements
Owner	1. Gradual sale of the company to employees for tax-deductible funds 2. Favorable tax treatment for reinvestment of proceeds into qualified replacement property (US stocks) 3. Retain control	1. Not available to sole proprietors and partnerships without changing the entity to a corporation 2. Intra-family and inter-generational stock transfers and ownership more difficult to structure with an ESOP

An ESOP creates a market for the shares of a privately held company, enabling an owner to retain control while selling ownership gradually to employees using tax-deductible company funds. Meanwhile employees gain ownership of the company they work for and a retirement fund, while putting up no cash.

The next article discusses techniques for using ESOPs to facilitate an owner's exit from the business.

16.2 Exit Strategy Techniques Using an Employee Stock Ownership Plan (ESOP)

Small business owners can use an ESOP to sell their business for its market value. They can do so gradually over time through regular annual tax-deductible company contributions to the ESOP, or in a single set of transactions using a "*leveraged ESOP*".

The ESOP then uses these funds to purchase shares from the company or from some or all of its stockholders.

Article 16.1 defined the advantages and disadvantages of an Employee Stock Ownership Plan (ESOP) for employees, the company, and the owner of a small business. In this article, we will consider how an owner can use a leveraged ESOP transaction to sell some or all of the owner's shares at once, as an *exit strategy* for the owner.

Leveraged ESOP Definition

A simple or basic ESOP uses regular annual company contributions to buy the company's stock. However, an ESOP can also borrow money to finance the purchase of shares of the company's stock. When it does so, it is referred to as a "leveraged ESOP."

While a "direct" loan to the ESOP might be appropriate in certain cases, banks more commonly prefer to lend funds to the company rather than directly to its ESOP. The company then relends the funds to the ESOP. This is sometimes called a "back-to-back loan," and the company's relending of the bank loan proceeds to the ESOP is called the "ESOP loan." Often, the ESOP Loan will have different repayment terms than the terms of the bank loan, such as lower interest rates and longer amortization.

Although beyond the scope of this article, it is worth noting that since the stock purchased by the ESOP is held in a "suspense account," it is allocated to participants' individual ESOP accounts only as the ESOP loan is repaid. Thus the company has the flexibility to structure the repayment period of the ESOP loan so as to provide equity ownership to employees who may be hired well into the future and not just to its current employees.

Use of Funds
The ESOP must use these borrowed funds solely to purchase "employer securities." In most privately held companies with only one class of shares outstanding, these will be the shares of the company's common stock.

When there is more than one class of common stock or series of preferred stock, the stock that can be purchased by the ESOP must have the "highest and best" dividend and voting rights of all classes of the company's stock.

ESOP Loan Repayment
The ESOP loan is repaid to the company using the annual tax-deductible contributions made from the company to the ESOP. These company contributions are then returned to the company in the form of payments on the ESOP loan.

The company is limited by federal tax law in the amount of tax-deductible contributions it can make to its qualified employee benefit plans (e.g., 401(k), profit sharing plans, ESOPs, etc.).

272 | *Business Techniques in Troubled Times: A Toolbox for Small Business Success*

The general limitation is 25 percent of a company's payroll per year. However, over and above this general 25 percent limitation, companies may make a contribution of an additional 25 percent of payroll per year if this additional contribution is used to fund the repayment of an ESOP loan.

Owner's Sale and Tax Benefits

The owner achieves the *maximum tax benefit* by selling at least 30 percent of his company stock to an ESOP and reinvesting the proceeds of his share sale into stocks and bonds of US companies (called "replacement property"), as noted in Article 16.1.

The share price that the ESOP pays to the owner for his shares cannot exceed the fair market value of the shares to be sold to the ESOP. An owner might receive a higher price by selling to an unrelated party (rather than to an ESOP) who, as a result of synergies gained from acquiring the company, might be willing to pay an acquisition premium, perhaps as high as 20 to 30 percent above the appraiser's determination of the fair market value of the shares if sold to an ESOP.

However, in such a non-ESOP sale, the purchase proceeds that the owner received would be subject to contemporaneous payment of federal and state income taxes. If that deal was structured as a "stock swap" to avoid such taxes, when the owner sold the buyer's stock to diversify, again federal and state income taxes would have to be paid.

In contrast, if the owner sold his shares to an ESOP, by complying with certain requirements, he or she would be able to defer and possibly avoid entirely paying any federal or state income taxes on the gain realized from the sale.

The "tax deferral" referred to above is only available to C corporations. Thus, if the company were an S corporation and wished to remain so, while ESOP solutions are still feasible, the owner's tax treatment might be less advantageous.

Maximum Tax Benefit: The "Home Run" Scenario

The "home run" transaction is for the owner of a C corporation to sell his or her shares to an ESOP, elect to defer taxes on the gain by reinvesting in qualified replacement property, and then have the company elect to be taxed as an S corporation after the transaction.

Why does this produce the maximum tax benefits? As we discussed in the previous article, an S corporation does not pay federal (and most state) income taxes. Instead, the income, losses, gains, etc., are "passed through" to the shareholders of the S corporation and they have to pay ordinary income tax on their share of the company's taxable income and gains.

Ordinarily, an S corporation would make a cash distribution to its shareholders that would, at a minimum, enable them to pay these taxes. However, the ESOP trust is a "tax exempt" entity. Thus, if the ESOP has purchased all the owners' shares and has itself become the owner of an S corporation, since the ESOP doesn't have to pay any federal (or most state) income taxes, the company would not have to make these annual cash distributions to the ESOP trust.

This cash would then be available for other corporate purposes, such as repaying the company's bank loans that funded the ESOP loan.

In this "home run" scenario, owners have sold the company and the ESOP is the new owner. The owners, if continuing to be actively employed, can continue to collect salaries (and bonuses). If they do not elect the "tax deferral" option, they can also participate in the ESOP on the same basis as all other employees.

If they elect the "tax deferral" option, they could choose to use the investment income earned on the "replacement property" purchased with their sale proceeds to supplement (or, if they do not remain actively employed, replace) the income they previously received from the company.

This extra cash retained by the company can be used to pay off debt, purchase appreciating property, make acquisitions and otherwise grow the company, or pay dividends to its owner the ESOP. All these uses increase the value of the shares in the individual employee ESOP accounts.

Getting Started with an ESOP

The main requirement to use a leveraged ESOP exit strategy is that the company (or the ESOP) has the credit capacity to get the loan to fund the large share purchase.

What steps would a small business owner take to find out if an ESOP exit strategy fits for him and his company? This quote from *"Using an Employee Stock Ownership Plan (ESOP) for Business Continuity in a Closely Held Company"*[42] sums up the process:

"Create an initial business plan, factoring in legal costs, the costs to buy the shares, and the company's cash flow. If that looks encouraging, talk to an accountant about your figures. If things still look promising, have a valuation done. Your valuation specialist will tell you how much your stock is worth and should also give you a more detailed idea about the practicality of selling these shares.

"If things still look good, hire a qualified ESOP attorney to draft your plan [*Editor's note*: and to help structure the ESOP transaction to fit with your objectives]. As you consider an ESOP, find some other ESOP company executives to talk to, attend an ESOP meeting or two, and finalize your plans with all the key players."

The next article summarizes the experience of one small business owner who sold his independent insurance agency to the company ESOP.

16.3 Lessons Learned from an ESOP Exit Experience

An independent insurance agency started its ESOP on January 1, 1994, to buy out a partner. Eventually the company sold itself to a third party in 2009. The experience of one of its owners adds some real-world context to the two preceding articles in this chapter.

General Comments:

- The company was always a C corporation. It had about 26 employees by the time it was sold.

- The ESOP was used twice to buy out departing shareowners.

- At the time of the sale in 2009, the ESOP already owned more than 50 percent of the company.

* The critical ingredient for having an ESOP is that the company must be profitable and generating enough cash to make annual contributions to the ESOP. In addition, if a leveraged ESOP is used, the company's credit must be good enough to merit a bank loan.

* An ESOP requires management attention from the owners, because it is a growing off-balance-sheet liability as profits grow and the percentage of vested shares increases. In addition, the ESOP must hold enough cash to fund anticipated redemptions, due to retirements and separations from service.

* The National Center for Employee Ownership (NCEO) focuses on smaller companies and thus was a more useful source of guidance than The ESOP Association, which gravitates toward larger company issues.[43]

* Establishing an ESOP does not prevent the company from having other benefit plans, such as stock options or a 401(k) plan, for some or all of the same people.

Setting Up the ESOP

* The setup process took about six months.

* Tasks included changing the corporate bylaws and the shareholder agreement, as well as establishing the ESOP trust.

* The cost in 1993 was, of course, less than today's cost. Then it was $25,000 to $30,000 for setup, $5,000 to $7,000 for the first year's administration, and $3,000 to $4,000 annually for administration in subsequent years, plus the time of one of the owners to function as internal overseer for ESOP matters.

- The need for internal administration becomes evident when one realizes that an ESOP is essentially a separate company with its own set of documents and its own manager (trustee).

Professional Administration

- It is important for the trustee to hire a professional ESOP administrator, because they are aware of the often-changing laws and regulations. Here is a comprehensive guide from one of them, Crowe Horwath: *Comprehensive Guide to ESOPs*.

- Annually, the shares purchased by the ESOP are assigned to individual employee accounts by this trustee as directed by the administrator.

- He or she also produces an annual statement of the ESOP's assets and changes to them, plus annual statements showing the balance of shares and cash in the individual employee accounts. In addition, the administrator accounts for all unallocated shares, held in a suspense account.

Control of the Business

- In general ESOP participants only vote on "major corporate issues," including merger, consolidation, recapitalization, reclassifications, liquidation, dissolution, and sale of substantially all of the assets of the business. In all other cases, the ESOP trustee votes the shares held by participants. The sale of the business to a third party was not deemed a "major corporate issue."

- Since shares were awarded based on compensation and years of employment, the vast majority of the shares were allocated to the accounts of the owners of the business. Thus, the owners remained in control.

Timing of Distribution Issues

- When the business was sold in 2009, only half the proceeds were distributed immediately after the sale. The rest were held pending Department of Labor approval for full distribution, in case any tax disputes required additional cash payments. That approval was expected to take twelve months but took twenty months instead due to DOL administrative errors.

- When two shareowners left the company, taking with them a significant amount of revenue, the attorney advised that a new appraisal of the value of the shares was needed, because the loss of those people caused the value of the business to decline. The resulting valuation was significantly less than the previous appraisal.

  Ten days after the departure of the shareholders, a third shareholder died, and the decedent's estate exercised their right to have the company buy back the decedent's shares at fair market value. The value was less than the day before the two shareholders departed.

  The company chose to use non-ESOP funds to repurchase the decedent shareholder's shares, but they were not *required* to do so. Also, they used the valuation prior to the two shareholders' departure. They were not *allowed* to pay more ESOP funds for the decedent's shares than the most recent appraised market value, so non-ESOP funds were needed to pay based on the pre-departure value.

Prior articles have shown that an ESOP can be a valuable tool, enabling owners of privately held companies to exit the business at a time of their choosing, while creating a retirement benefit for employees and a better cash position for the company. This article shows that those benefits come with some cost and complexity, requiring management, like any other major company initiative.

Distressed Businesses

D ISTRESSED BUSINESSES are those that are running out of cash. Often they believe that growth—more customers—is the answer. But serving more customers with unprofitable products, inefficient processes, wasted resources, and unfocused management does not change the fundamental cause of distress. Business distress requires a review of the business model, marketing, and operations, all under the pressure of seemingly impossible cash demands.

Part Six's Driving Concepts

- Businesses that get into trouble usually realize it too late. They have not been analyzing their numbers and creating improvements.

- A distressed business has three choices: fix it, sell it, or close it. Not all businesses are candidates for the "fix it" option. But *doing nothing* is not an option.

- An outside perspective is required to choose the right option and drive implementation. Owners who got into this situation rarely have the skills to get out of it without help.

- Your turnaround advisor will first do a general review of the business to find the weak areas. Every weakness is an opportunity to improve. Then detailed analysis homes in on specific issues, resulting in a set of major improvement projects. The question is: who has the time, skills, and energy to make them happen?

- Lender forbearance or even bankruptcy may be a tool to buy time for these improvements to show results. More lender negotiation and alternate financing techniques will be presented in 2013 articles on the blog *Business Techniques in Troubled Times*.

Techniques Presented in Part Six

Topic	Techniques	Content	Articles
Situation Analysis	General Situation Analysis	Business model; P&L; trends; competitive analysis; SWOT; goals	17.1
	Detailed Situation Analysis	Overhead; process efficiency; product profitability; customer profitability; marketing and sales; organization	17.2
	Implementation Planning	Management competence; gap analysis and management skills; owner goals	17.3
	Bankruptcy	Benefits; costs; decision considerations; counsel	17.4

Chapter 17: Situation Analysis and Bankruptcy

17.1 Fixing a Troubled Company: Where to Start?

The first phase in fixing a troubled company is called "*situation analysis.*" Not a catchy name, is it? Maybe a better name would be "forensic management" or "what's going on here?" We cannot change the name, but we *can* learn how to use this technique.

In practice, this process has three parts: general, detailed, and deciding-what-to-do-next. Whether you are the owner, an investor, a buyer, or a "turnaround consultant," the analysis process is the same.

The General Stage

In the general stage, you start with the question "what do we have here?" You are trying to understand the "big picture" before you break it down into parts and analyze each of them. Experience suggests that we look at the business six different ways in this general stage of situation analysis:

1. Business Model: How does the business make money today? It gathers some *inputs*, such as raw materials, skilled labor, the right machinery, and proprietary information. Then it somehow *processes* the inputs to create some *output* that customers find attractive. What are the inputs? What are the processes? What are the outputs? Are customers paying more for the outputs than the business paid to create them? If not, you don't have a business!

2. Income Statement (P&L): How much money does the business make today? What products produce most of its revenue? What cost elements eat up most of those revenues? Does it make enough money today to justify the risk of being in business? For the last few years, has the profit trend been flat, up, or down?

3. Trends in the Market: What do outside developments suggest about the business's prospects for future profits? They might create opportunities or threats. Use the acronym DPEST to remind yourself to consider demographic, political/regulatory, economic, socio-cultural, and technology trends.

After considering these general trends, think about specific trends in the industry itself, concerning customers, competitors, suppliers, sales channels, and technology. Again, these trends might create opportunities or threats.

For an example of using trends, consider this. Smaller households and female participation in the workforce are demographic trends that imply it is becoming more common that no one is home to accept a delivery. This can be a threat to Amazon's reputation for delivery excellence, but their recent initiative for drop-boxes in convenience stores is a great response.

Amazon's competitors who own retail stores can offer the option to have online orders delivered to stores for later pickup, rather than to homes. Amazon had no way to compete with this advantage because they did not have their own stores, until they created their drop-box initiative using rented wall space.

The analyst asks, "Which trends will affect the business, and is this business in a position to benefit from the trend, or be hurt by it?" Ideally, you want your business to be on the right side of major trends, gaining as the trends continue, rather than fighting to hold back a tide that will eventually happen no matter what you do.

4. Competitive Analysis: Why do my prospects choose my competitor instead? For a simple matrix to use for competitive analysis, see Chapter 3. The Competitive Analysis Matrix assesses the company vs. competitors according to what criteria the customers consider when they are making the buying decision. See the author's short video on using this technique at *http://www .youtube.com/watch?v=Cgxx9Qf-9wk*.[44]

Additional questions reveal something about the "staying power" of competitors. How do my competitors make money (their business model)? Will the trends have the same effect on them as they will on me, or will I be better or worse off?

5. SWOT (strengths, weaknesses, opportunities, threats): We already considered trends to find the *external* opportunities and threats. Strengths and weaknesses are found by *internal* analysis. Examples include the strength of your brand, financial strength, operational processes, employee skills, location, repeat customers, computer system, marketing program, unique products, and the like. SWOT is summarized by short bullet items in a table like this:

Internal	Strengths:	Weaknesses:
	• item • item • item	• item • item • item
External	Opportunities:	Threats:
	• item • item • item	• item • item • item

6. Goals: What are the owner's goals for himself or herself and for the business? Does he want to exit soon with cash flow for retirement? Does he want to build a powerhouse? Does he just want to stay small enough for a comfortable business and a comfortable cash flow? Does he want to sell?

Now we know enough about the business in general to understand its size, its financial and competitive position, how customers see it, its challenges, and how the owner would like to see its future. This enables the detailed part of situation analysis.

The analyst must recognize that this first stage can create some discomfort and impatience: the owner has never thought about the business in these ways; the financial and other data is not readily available; the outcome of the analysis may contradict the owner's long-held views; he is paying you for positive changes, not for wordy analyses. Discomfort easily becomes frustration, which can quickly transition to impatience!

The analyst must resist the temptation to respond to owner impatience by choosing a course of action too soon, after only a general review of the business. The best antidote to the owner's impatience is always speedy analysis. See the next article for the next steps.

17.2 Fixing a Troubled Company: The Detailed Phase

The preceding article on "situation analysis" defined the starting point: a general analysis of the company in terms of business model, profit and loss statement, trends, competitive analysis, SWOT, and owner's goals.

The second stage of "situation analysis" looks deeper into how the company tries to make a profit, assessing how well it is performing in those efforts. This enables the third stage, where the analyst and the owner/manager select a course of action.

The Overriding Question

In this deeper look, the overriding question is, "Can you make something that enough customers want, and make it better or at lower cost than competitors so the customer is willing to pay a price that yields enough profit?"

If not, you need to reconsider products and the process for making them (see Chapters 10 and 13: product strategy and process improvement). Otherwise, if you *can* make these products that customers find valuable, then the focus will be on getting more such customers at the right price (see Chapters 8, 9, and 10: pricing, sales, and marketing communications).

The Detailed Analysis Stage

We look at the business seven ways to make this detailed situation analysis:

1. Fixed Costs or Overhead: These are the costs that do not change regardless of the number of sales and amount of sales revenue. They include rent, utilities, systems costs, machine and (some) maintenance costs, marketing, nonproductive employee time, and others.

Usually small business owners have an excellent handle on overhead costs, with the possible exception of nonproductive employee time. This is the cost of wages for time *not* spent working on revenue-producing production. While it includes paid absence, the main issue is paid time when the employee is between jobs (in a job shop). If it is 20 percent, that's normal. If it is 40 percent, that is not good!

Owners may not have quantified this time because they haven't measured how much time employees spend being productive. If there is no system for tracking hours spent per job, then the owner and the analyst should estimate it by type of job or product. They have to do this anyway for the product profitability analysis (see below).

2. Process Efficiency: The calculation here is the number or value of the outputs (products, subassemblies, or parts) divided by the number or value of the inputs (raw materials, labor hours, other).

For example, a restaurant could measure wait staff productivity in meals served per labor hour. Cooking productivity might be meals revenue per hour divided by the hourly labor cost of the cook plus average cost of the ingredients used per hour.

Once you have an efficiency measurement, you can compare it to industry averages obtained from a trade association, or to best-in-class operators ("benchmarking"). This tells us how efficient your process is vs. competitors, and it may explain one important reason why your costs are higher than theirs.

Quality is an issue here as well. Your cost measurement should consider the cost of rejects. Perhaps higher quality is a reason to accept higher process costs, but *only* if customers are willing to pay a premium price for that quality.

3. Product Profitability: Price minus the variable cost of producing the product yields product profitability, called gross margin or contribution margin.

Variable means those costs that do not happen if the product is not produced. They include raw materials, productive labor hours, any production-related outside contractor costs, plus delivery and sales commission costs. We assume at this point that all labor costs are variable.

If your product profitability is less than 50 percent (i.e., if price is not double the variable cost), you are likely to have trouble covering your overhead while still making a profit, depending on your industry. The price we use here is the price you charge to the next layer in the value chain. For example, if you sell to distributors, use the price you charge them, not the retail price.

When the company is a "job shop," making a variety of products customized for each order, the owner will be asked to identify job types rather than products. Usually there will be three: a simple repetitive order, an order of average complexity, and a major customized project.

The product profitability analysis often shows that the price is too low because it does not cover all the hours spent, or does not produce enough margin to cover overhead, including non-productive wages.

4. Customer Profitability: Some segments of customers (type of business, region, age, or some other distinguishing characteristic) simply will not pay enough to yield target profits, for reasons that may include competition, late payments, too many change orders, or too much customization. Other customer segments are your sweet spot: pleased with your quality and willing to pay for it.

Customer profitability should drive your marketing effort. You want to attract more who are in the sweet spot and decline to serve those who do not yield enough profit. See Articles 10.5 and 10.6, and Chapter 15 on the customer database.

5. Marketing Program: The competitive analysis (see prior article) highlighted your "differentiation." The customer profitability analysis identified your best types of customers.

The marketing program starts with deciding how you want these "best customers" to think of your company/products—your positioning. Maybe it is innovative solutions. Or maybe it is reliability and quality. Whatever it is, your marketing program must then be designed to reinforce this positioning to these types of prospects. Using the famous four Ps, ask yourself:

- Can I change the *product* to fit my positioning better and to fit better with the needs of these prospects? Should I come up with something new?

- Does my *pricing* approach support the image I want to have in the minds of these prospects, or should I tweak it? Would they pay a little more? If so, that small price increase can give profits a major boost. See Article 8.4.

- Can they find my product in a *place* they like to shop and one that fits my positioning? Should I find new distributors or new retail outlets? Is my web presence all it could be? Am I using social media well? How good is my sales force coverage? Could I improve my sales support? See Article 9.6.

- Do my *communications* reach the target customers when they are ready to buy? Are my *promotions* designed to fit my positioning? Do they get the attention of the target prospects? Do they value my promotions? If not, what should I do differently?

6. Sales Channels: Do I have my sales resources targeted at these highly desirable prospects, or are they going after easy low-margin sales? If it's the latter, how can I change sales force behavior: compensation plan, management, training, more coverage, the use of sales agents or distributors, or better sales support?

7. Organization: Do I have my resources aligned to my priorities? Often a small business knows what to do but is unwilling to hire the expertise to make it happen. They tend to load transformational projects on the shoulders of one or two key managers who are already working more than full time on day-to-day responsibilities.

In that case, the near term always drives out the long term so the changes that can save the business never get done because the big change projects are starved for resources.

This detailed situation analysis provides the information needed to decide what can be done about the business. The final step, covered in the next article, is deciding what to do next—where do we go from here?

17.3 After Situation Analysis: Where Do We Go from Here?

There are only three choices for a troubled business: fix it, sell it, or close it. Situation analysis tells you about the business today, but you need some more thinking to use that information to decide what to do with your troubled business tomorrow.

Now that you have done general and detailed situation analysis as in Articles 17.1 and 17.2, you can answer three critical questions:

1. Is there a viable core business?

2. Capital: is there adequate "bridge" financing until the business can support itself?

3. Is there a capable management team?

The Turnaround Management Association calls these the three Cs: core, capital, competence. If there is no viable core business—if enough customers are not willing to pay a profitable price for what it does—then your options are reduced to two: sell it or close it. The same two options apply if the necessary capital is not available.

Competent Management and Vision
When the problem seems to be competent management, one must ask, "Competent to do what?" The first response is: competent to run the projects needed to transform the business. But we don't yet know what the transformed business would look like, and so we don't yet know what those projects are! How do we determine that?

Start with dreaming. The owner and his or her advisors should create a vision of the business three years from now. The form of the vision is a brief statement about five to ten key aspects of the business—this is the description of the transformed business.

Some examples of these key aspects are revenue, customers, products, competitive position, brand identity, infrastructure/facilities, key processes, distribution channels, level of profit, and others. Place yourself in the future, and make a statement of what it is *at that time.*

For example, our revenue is xyz, most of our customers are (describe them), and they buy from us because we do (this) better than the competition, etc.

For some details on how to go about it, see Chapter 1.

Gap Analysis and Management Skills
Once you have a vision and you have completed situation analysis, you can identify the gaps between where the business is going

and where it is today. This "gap analysis" easily translates into a list of key projects needed to transform the business.

Now you can identify the management skills needed to carry out those projects. Decide whether the current team has the necessary competence. If not, consultants and/or hiring are options, plus training the current staff.

These alternatives are not free, of course. Perhaps more capital will be needed than originally thought. So now that we know what needs to be done, it is time to revisit the questions of adequate capital and competent management.

Owner Goals

If capital can be found and management is adequate or can be augmented, the owner must decide if he or she wants to make the effort to "turnaround" the business rather than sell it or close it. So this is the point where you do another "revisit." Think again about the owner's goals, once you know the work involved in the turnaround. Does he or she still want to tackle it, or does he or she prefer to find an exit?

If the owner decides to take on the turnaround challenge, an action plan is required—a set of project plans with interim targets and assigned resources. Lenders will want to see these specifics and projected financials for the entire turnaround period, probably monthly at least for the first year.

Why Not Just "Make Do"

As noted in other articles, when turnaround plans fail, the reason is often that managers already working more than full time on day-to-day issues are assigned to implement transformation projects as well, so they just don't get done! Management resources are a critical element of these plans. Do we have the right resources? If not, when will we get them? Be sure to include their costs.

Hiring new resources to manage new work seems obvious but costly. But the alternative to these costs is "sell it or close it," not "make do." Lenders may require that a "turnaround manager" be hired, or that the management team be augmented with people who have the missing skills, or that you hire people to take over the responsibilities of current managers so they can be free to work on the new projects.

I provide turnaround consulting advice. In addition, for free advice on turning around your business, contact the Pro Bono Committee of the Turnaround Management Association in your area or your local SCORE chapter. In the Chicago area, you can reach them at these links:

TMA Pro Bono: *http://www.turnaround.org/cmaextras/ TMAProBonoOverviewandApplicationv03.pdf*

SCORE west, northwest, and south: *www.scorefoxvalley.org*

SCORE central and north: *SCORE Chicago – Counseling, workshops, advice and business plans*[45]

17.4 Can Small Businesses Benefit from a Chapter 11 Bankruptcy?

By guest author Barbara Yong, Partner at Golan & Christie, a Chicago law firm

The answer is a resounding, *YES!* Here are the benefits of bankruptcy:

1. Immediately upon filing, the debtor is entitled to the protections of the *automatic stay.* This prevents your creditors from taking any action to collect their debts. It puts all litigation on hold and can prevent a lender from proceeding with a foreclosure of its mortgage or a UCC sale of business assets. This is meant to afford you a little bit of breathing room.

2. The debtor can also *reject unfavorable contracts* like leases or rental agreements. This allows you to close locations and get relief from above market rent.

3. The debtor can also borrow new money through a debtor-in-possession or *DIP loan*, and give the lender a super-priority lien, which puts them ahead of the business' existing lenders.

4. Debtors can also *sell some or all of their assets* free and clear of liens and claims, with the liens attaching to the proceeds of the sale. This can include real estate, machinery and equipment, vehicles, and even intellectual property.

5. The debtor also gets a *reprieve from paying its prebankruptcy debts* while it is in Chapter 11. During this time, the debtor can accumulate a surplus to help strengthen the business after

bankruptcy. While these debts must be addressed in a plan and a percentage must be paid over time, the total to be paid to unsecured creditors depends on the liquidation value of the business, which is generally much less than the total owed.

Can some or all of this be done outside of a bankruptcy? The answer is no. These protections only exist in bankruptcy.

How Should I Decide about Bankruptcy?

Is Chapter 11 the answer for every small business that either can't afford to pay its creditors or finds itself upside down, meaning its liabilities exceed its assets? The answer is no, but it should definitely be considered, along with several other less costly options.

These options should be discussed with experienced bankruptcy counsel, especially if the business is continuing to lose money and can only survive by increasing the amounts owed to its trade creditors or by failing to pay payroll taxes, both of which can subject the business owner to personal liability.

Some of the factors for or against the filing of a bankruptcy include the following:

* Whether the business can break even or operate at a profit *during* the Chapter 11

* Whether the business model is effective (e.g., do they offer goods and/or services that are in demand?)

* What is the relationship between the debtor and its trade creditors?

* What is the relationship between the debtor and its lenders?

- Does the business own the real estate in which it operates and, if not, what is the relationship between the debtor and its landlord?

- What is the quality and loyalty of the workforce?

- Does the owner have access to cash or credit to put into the business?

- Does the business have nonessential assets that can be marketed and sold?

- Did the business owners take a lot of money out of the business during the prior year?

And there are many others.

Oh, don't get me wrong; it is definitely *possible* for struggling and cash-strapped businesses to change their business model, obtain new financing, restructure existing debt, and negotiate payment plans with their creditors without filing a bankruptcy.

My firm and I offer these services to our clients, as do the many highly experienced turnaround consultants and professionals who also belong to the Turnaround Management Association (TMA). But when all else fails, Chapter 11 should at least be considered as an option before shutting the doors.

Cost of Bankruptcy

While Chapter 11 is expensive, don't let the price tag deter you. Yes, there are debtor counsel fees, lender counsel fees, quarterly trustee fees, and sometimes even creditor committee fees. But depending on the size of the business, these fees are quite reasonable compared to the valuable benefits Chapter 11 can provide, not to mention the huge amount of debt that can be eliminated from your business's bottom line.

Experience Counts!

Why should you believe all this? Guest author Barb Yong has been practicing law for 30 years and bankruptcy for nearly 20. Most of her experience comes from representing small businesses and business owners.

She is also a board member and officer of the Chicago/Midwest Chapter of the Turnaround Management Association (TMA) and a founding member of the Chicago Network of the International Women's Insolvency and Restructuring Confederation (IWIRC).

Plus, her firm, Golan & Christie, currently has the most active Chapter 11 cases pending in the Northern District of Illinois.

Contact Barb Yong at *Blyong@golanchristie.com* to see whether your business might benefit from filing a Chapter 11 bankruptcy or one of the less costly alternatives.

Conclusion

THIS BOOK STARTED WITH the uplifting process of "Imagining Excellence," envisioning your business three years from now. We started on that very positive note, but the book ended on the subject of distressed businesses, turnaround, and bankruptcy! Is this depressing spiral the fate of most small businesses?

Of course not! If it was, the courts would be swamped and the consulting industry and turnaround firms would be as rich as tort lawyers and hedge funds! The problems leading to a turnaround are troublesome, but the turnaround process itself is the path from weakness to strength and success.

As Winston Churchill said, "Difficulties mastered are opportunities won."

Small business owners face "difficulties" every day, as they pursue of their dream of achieving independence by bringing value to customers. Owners face decisions and risk, and they do it mostly alone.

People are always around, but there is no one else to make the decision for you and often no confidante who understands the business well enough to deliver the solution. Advisors are expensive, and you fear their advice is too general to be worth the money.

Plus, let's not forget who these owners are. They are independent and self-motivated, so they may not listen very well to advice!

This book provides the trusted outside perspective that small business decision-makers have been missing. It collects and explains practical techniques to help small businesses make the right decisions, based on 40 years of management and consulting experience. This book is designed to be your toolbox and guide to "master difficulties and win opportunities."

See the following few pages for a full list of the techniques presented in this book. I hope you find at least some of them useful in your business! If you do, please keep up to date with *new* blog articles published weekly on Business Techniques in Troubled Times. Sign up for weekly emails of fresh articles at *www.tom-gray.com/blog-2/*.

Herb Kelleher, former CEO of Southwest Airlines, has a great quote to take us from considering to doing: "We have a strategic plan. It's called doing things."

So do some things to make your business better!

Share what works by posting a comment on the blog, and contact Tom Gray at *tgray@tom-gray.com* for personal advice on techniques to solve your business problems.

Index of Topics and Techniques

Topic	Technique	Content	Articles
Vision	Imagining Excellence	Describe company in three years; multiple facets	1.1-1.3
	Gaining Buy-In	Leadership techniques for gaining commitment	1.4
	Nine-Cell Decision Matrix	Prioritization in a group setting	1.5
Business Planning	Business Plan Structure	Simple plan outline	2.1
	Market Analysis	Trends, target market, competitors	2.2, 2.7
	Competitive Analysis and Matrix	Assessing competitors for how well they meet prioritized customer buying criteria	3.1-3.2
	Competitive Analysis, Differentiation and Positioning	Finding and expressing your competitive edge	2.2, 3.1
	Market Sizing	Using databases to profile competitors and size market segments	2.8
	Sales Funnel and Sales Cycle	Realistic views of the sales effort, revenue timing, and sales force sizing	4.1-4.2
	Marketing Planning	Product offers, pricing, sales, communications, customer service to support positioning	2.3
	Sales Forecasting	Methods and mechanics	2.4, 4.2
	Forecasting Cash Flow	Methods and mechanics	2.5, 4.2
	Cash Cycle	Realistic timing for costs vs. revenue	2.5, 4.2
	Presenting the Financial Plan	Summarizing the spreadsheets in your business plan	2.5

Financing with Debt	Becoming an Attractive Borrower	Resources; loan uses; are you a good risk?	5.1
	Community Bank Lending Criteria	Goals; banker's basic questions/criteria; documents needed	5.2
	SBA Loans	Top SBA lenders; eligibility; loan types/terms	5.3
	Microloans	Lenders; size and terms; eligibility and uses; peer-to-peer lending	5.4
	Asset-Based Lending (ABL)	Types of collateral; interest rates; sources	5.5
	Understanding Lender Remedies	Early, middle, and late stage lender techniques and borrower responses	5.6
Financing with Equity	Understanding Angel Investors	Who are angel investors; what types of businesses; terms; other benefits; sources	6.1
	Investing with Family	Business plan analysis; bases for assumptions; working capital; profit distribution; valuation	6.2
	Managing Risk in Family Investment	Types of risk; shareholder agreement; supermajority rights; dispute resolution; exit provisions	6.3
Product Strategy	Three Tiers	Bundles of features	7.1
	Augmented Product	Packaging, warranties, ancillary services	7.1
	Service Design	Design the customer experience according to positioning	7.2
	Product Roadmap	New product schedule according to customer segment needs	7.3

Sales	Insight Selling	Types of target companies; "insight" approach; internal allies; sales approach	9.3
	Sales Compensation	Target compensation; salary vs. commission; bonus; promotions (SPIFF)	9.4
	Segmented Compensation	Different incentives for stars, core performers, and laggards	9.5
	Sales Support	Five "helpers" and nine "tools"	9.6
Market Communications	Market Communications (Marcom) Planning	Target audience; different tools for different goals; budgeting techniques	10.1
	Traditional Media	Choose the media that fits the communications task	10.2
	Website Design	Site planning; page planning; content writing; professional designer; updating	10.3
	Using Social Media	Sequence of social media; content selection and calendar	10.4
	Customer Database Design	Purposes; data to capture; operations and data entry process	10.5
	Customer Database Reports and Record Design	Envision reports; design their content; then design customer data record to fit how reports will use the data	10.6
	Roadmap for Marketing	Summary of marketing articles with graphic	10.7
Using Your Numbers	Useful P&L Format	Group accounts into a few categories	11.1
	P&L Analysis	Prioritize by percentage of revenue	11.1, 11.2
	Profit Improvement	Drop low-margin products; reduce costs; raise prices	11.2

Thirteen Week Cash Flow Statement	Design Thirteen Week Cash Flow Statement	This is the owner's job; statement design	12.1
	Forecasting Cash	Forecasting knowns and unknowns	12.2, 12.3
	Assessing Cash Flow	Split labor cost; reasonableness check; shop rate	12.4
Process Improvement	Process Map	Understand the process before changing it; some mechanics	13.1
	Big Picture Process Improvement	Limit options; self-perform; resequence; hand-offs; subassembly; computer support	13.2
	Step Analysis Process Improvement	Better equipment; more efficient methods; fail-safe methods; people management; measurements and standards	13.3
Family Employees	Family Employee Issues	Skills; behavior; expectations	14.1
	Using Policies to Manage	Job descriptions; market-based compensation	14.2
	Management Techniques for Family Employees	Values statement; objectives and accountability; major project approval policy	14.3
Growth through Focus: Pruning	Segment by Margin	Segmentation; focus on winners	15.1
	Pruning Process	Nine steps; what can go wrong; old way/new way	15.2
Employee Stock Ownership Plans	Simple ESOP	Definition; distributions; control; costs; tax benefits; advantages/disadvantages	16.1
	Leveraged ESOP	Definition; use of funds; loan; structure and benefits; getting started	16.2
	ESOP Lessons Learned	Company administration; setup time/cost; professional administration; control; distribution issue	16.3

Situation Analysis	General Situation Analysis	Business model; P&L; trends; competitive analysis; SWOT; goals	17.1
	Detailed Situation Analysis	Overhead; process efficiency; product profitability; customer profitability; marketing and sales; organization	17.2
	Implementation Planning	Management competence; gap analysis and management skills; owner goals	17.3
	Bankruptcy	Benefits; costs; decision considerations; counsel	17.4

References

1 *http://www.sba.gov* and *http://dor.wa.gov/docs/reports/ BusinessSurvivalReportOct2007.pdf.*

2 George Harrison (*http://www.goodreads.com/quotes/tag/ direction*) quoting Lewis Carroll's *Alice in Wonderland*.

3 *"An Operational Turnaround's First 100 Days,"* Thomas H. Gray, previously published in The Turnaround Management Association's *Journal for Corporate Renewal*.

4 Fournies, Ferdinand F., *Why Employees Don't Do What They're Supposed to Do and What to Do About It*, McGraw-Hill, 1999.

5 *"Competitive Analysis: Find Your Edge,"* YouTube, *http://www.youtube.com/watch?v=Cgxx9Qf-9wk.*

6 *http://www.scorefoxvalley.org/business_planning.php.*

7 Ewing Marion Kauffman Foundation quoted in the *Wall Street Journal*, November 12, 2012.

8 *"Competitive Analysis: Find Your Edge,"* YouTube, *http://www.youtube.com/watch?v=Cgxx9Qf-9wk.*

9 *http://marketingartfully.com/2011/03/15/small-business- lead-generating-sales-funnel/.*

10 *http://www.scorefoxvalley.org/images/uploads/15%20 SOURCES%20OF%20FINANCING.pdf.*

11 Ewing Marion Kauffman Foundation quoted in the *Wall Street Journal*, November 12, 2012.

12 *http://www.score.org/resources/grants-non-profits.*

13 *http://www.scorefoxvalley.org/images/uploads/F5%20 Qualifying%20For%20A%20Loan.pdf.*

14 *http://www.scorefoxvalley.org/images/uploads/F1%20The%20 ABCs%20Of%20Borrowing.pdf.*

15 *Small Business Loans : Financial & Business Advice : Accion East and Online* and *http://www.sba.gov/content/ microloan-program.*

16 Light, Joe, "Would You Lend Money to These People?" *Wall Street Journal*, April 13, 2012.

17 This article is based in large part on *"Alternative Financing Sources Options for Challenging Situations," Turnaround Management Association*, by Tom Goldblatt, CTP, Monomoy Capital Partners.

18 Ibid.

19 This article is based in large part on *"Lender Remedies: Reading Between the Lines," Turnaround Management Association*, by Bobby Guy, *The Journal for Corporate Renewal*, April 2012.

20 Kauffmann Foundation at *http://www.entrepreneurship. org/en/Resource-Center/Topics/Accounting-and-Finance. aspx* and the Angel Investor Association at *http://www. angelcapitalassociation.org/.*

21 *http://www.godaddy.com/hosting/web-hosting.aspx?ci= 8971.*

22 *Operations Management,* by Jay Heizer and Barry Render, Prentice Hall, 2011, Tenth Edition, page 158.

23 *http://www.entrepreneur.com/article/206390.*

24 *http://www.youtube.com/watch?v=JhjUJTw2i1M.*

25 *http://smallbusiness.chron.com/average-profit-margin wholesale-12941.html.*

26 *http://travi.st/2009/09/pricing-markup-margins-and-mass-confusion/.*

27 *http://hbsp.harvard.edu/multimedia/flashtools/channel margins/index.html.*

28 *http://www.openforum.com/idea-hub/topics/money/article/ understanding-the-economics-of-your-product-distribution-channels-1/.*

29 *www.tsnn.com.*

30 Modern Distribution Management at *http://www.mdm .com/,* the National Association of Wholesaler-Distributors (NAW) at *http://www.naw.org/,* or *http://www.tradepub .com/* and websites like *http://www.ezgoo.com/.*

31 *http://www.gale.cengage.com/DirectoryLibrary/GML 33507EA%20GDL.pdf* and *http://www.asaecenter.org/.*

32 This article is based in large part on "The End of Solution Sales," by Brent Adamson, Matthew Dixon, and Nicholas Toman, *Harvard Business Review,* July/August 2012.

[33] This article is based in large part on "Motivating Salespeople: What Really Works," by Thomas Steenburgh and Michael Ahearne, *Harvard Business Review*, July/August 2012.

[34] *"Tweet Me, Friend Me, Make Me Buy," by Barbara Giamanco and Kent Gregoire,* Harvard Business Review, July/August 2012.

[35] *http://www.copyblogger.com/brainstorm-blog-topics/.*

[36] *https://www.facebook.com/help/389849807718635/.*

[37] "13-Week Cash Flow Model Creates Clear Communication Channels," by Ray Anderson, Frank R. Mack, Ronald J. Reuter, and Anu R. Singh, *The Journal of Corporate Renewal,* Turnaround Management Association, July 1, 2006, *http://www.turnaround.org/Publications/Articles.aspx?objectID=6297.*

[38] *http://www.balancedscorecard.org/Portals/0/PDF/bpihndbk.pdf.*

[39] This article is based in large part on *"Growth through Focus: A Blueprint for Driving Profitable Expansion,"* by Khosla and Sawhney in *Strategy and Business*, Autumn 2010.

[40] Ibid

[41] *https://www.nceo.org/.*

[42] "Using an Employee Stock Ownership Plan (ESOP) for Business Continuity in a Closely Held Company," *http://www.nceo.org/articles/esop-business-continuity.*

[43] *https://www.nceo.org/* and *http://www.esopassociation.org/.*

[44] *http://www.youtube.com/watch?v=Cgxx9Qf-9wk.*

[45] For free turnaround resources, see

TMA Pro Bono: *http://www.turnaround.org/cmaextras/TMAProBonoOverviewandApplicationv03.pdf.*

SCORE in the west, northwest, and south suburbs of Chicago: *www.scorefoxvalley.org.*

SCORE in Chicago and its north suburbs: *SCORE Chicago—Counseling, workshops, advice, and business plans.*

About the Author

Tom Gray helps owners save and grow their companies. He is a management consultant focused on small business and telecom, a Certified Turnaround Professional (CTP), a Certified Business Development Advisor, a Certified SCORE Mentor, and adjunct professor of business. His career experience includes large companies and small, including his own consulting firm. He held positions as President, Interim CEO, Vice President, General Manager, and member of the Board of Directors. He can be reached at *tgray@tom-gray.com*. See *www.tom-gray.com*. Tom and his wife Nancy live in Lisle, Illinois.